"If you are like me, you love to be given a front-row seat, a back-stage pass, or that red-carpet invitation! I had the honor of seeing this book, and the TV series that inspired it, blossom from a seed to an amazing, beautiful adventure because its very talented creator, Rebecca, took a few weeks in her travels to edit and do a few photo shoots from my home. Not only did Rebecca find beauty all over the world, she teamed with God to create beauty wherever she traveled! This book will create beauty in your life and will give you the tips and tools to paint a path of beauty wherever you travel too!"

Pam Farrel, bestselling author of *Men Are Like Waffles—Women Are Like Spaghetti* and *7 Simple Skills for Every Woman*

"'God is the Author of beautiful stories.' We want that to be true, and it is. It is Rebecca's heart that you'd discover your own gifts and value through her powerful images of beautifully diverse women and breathtaking stories, shattering the lies of the enemy with the turn of each page in her new book—and I believe you will."

Andi Andrew, author, speaker, copastor of Liberty Church, and founder of She Is Free

"*Finding Beautiful* is a wonderful book full of intriguing stories that reveal the miracle of the Father's love for His daughters. As my friend Rebecca takes you on a journey around the world, she unearths truths about real, genuine beauty that point us toward the redeeming love of the Father. You will love these stories and find new ways to show your unique beauty to those you love and make your mark on the world with the internal attributes that truly make a woman beautiful. Thank you, Rebecca, for sharing your amazing journey with us and pointing us always toward the beauty of a life led by none other than the Author of beauty Himself, Jesus."

Jennifer Strickland, author of *Beautiful Lies, Girl Perfect,* and *More Beautiful Than You Know;* former professional model; speaker; and founder of URMore.org

"From California to Paris, Rebecca Friedlander has searched for stories of true beauty. Not stories of glitz and glamour but stories of women who know their identity in Christ and have let their beauty overflow to those around them. Pick up this book to re-define your own beauty and learn how to share it with others."

Shannon Ethridge, MA, life/relationship coach, international speaker, and author of the million-copy bestselling Every Woman's Battle series

"Transformation is God's idea. But Rebecca Friedlander has shown with clarity that the will to change is ours alone. With before-and-after pictures that speak a thousand words, compelling testimonies, and thought-provoking questions that will ignite your own transformation, *Finding Beautiful* is unlike any other book I've ever seen. Can I be next? Will you?"

Laura Harris Smith, CNC; author, *Seeing the Voice of God, The 30-Day Faith Detox, The Healthy Living Handbook,* and *Get Well Soon;* host, *theTHREE*

FINDING

Beautiful

DISCOVERING
AUTHENTIC BEAUTY
AROUND THE WORLD

REBECCA FRIEDLANDER

BakerBooks

a division of Baker Publishing Group
Grand Rapids, Michigan

Published by Baker Books
a division of Baker Publishing Group
PO Box 6287, Grand Rapids, MI 49516-6287
www.bakerbooks.com

Printed in the United States of America

Library of Congress Cataloging-in-Publication Data
Names: Friedlander, Rebecca, 1980– author.
Title: Finding beautiful : discovering authentic beauty around the world / Rebecca Friedlander.
Description: Grand Rapids, MI : Baker Books, a division of Baker Publishing Group, [2019]
Identifiers: LCCN 2018045144 | ISBN 9780801093838 (cloth)
Subjects: LCSH: Aesthetics—Religious aspects—Christianity. | Christian women—Religious aspects.
Classification: LCC BR115.A8 F75 2019 | DDC 248.8/43—dc23
LC record available at https://lccn.loc.gov/2018045144

The author is represented by the William K. Jensen Literary Agency.

19   20   21   22   23   24   25   7   6   5   4   3   2   1

To my friend and mentor Pam Farrel,

a beautiful soul who encouraged my dreams.

Thank you for following hard after Jesus

and investing your life into women

around the world.

Contents

Introduction

What would it look like to pack your bags and travel the world in search of true beauty? If you wanted to document authentic beauty, would you capture fashion models on runways, nature's finest mountaintops, a mother's arms, or intriguing corners of the globe that most people ignore? I did it all in a nine-month adventure from Paris to Los Angeles, styling makeovers and photo shoots with fascinating women who shared powerful discoveries about passion, faith, and beauty. I found that many lies women mistakenly believe about their identity are often similar, regardless of their background or nationality, and that each radiant truth also has a common theme. This book is your personal ticket to adventure and a daring quest to discover your identity as a woman of God! Let's travel together—meeting new friends, styling great makeovers, and learning what God's Word teaches about timeless beauty.

As we start this adventure, let me explain what motivated my journey. As a film director, I was hired to produce a documentary that pulled back the sleek veneer of today's fashion industry. According to the *New York Post*, a survey conducted of over three thousand models from every major agency concluded that 94 percent are "woefully underweight."* Eating disorders and competition abound as the world's "most beautiful" vie for the next job and strive for the unattainable mirage of perfection. Even when a model gets a job, she is simply considered a performer for the photographer. In fact, the word for "model" in French is *le mannequin,* meaning "mannequin." Like an expendable droid in a sci-fi movie, she is easily replaced by the next girl waiting to fill her shoes. One former model told me through her tears, "I felt like a piece of meat in a butcher's shop window . . . just a piece of flesh to be haggled over. Was this really all there was to life?"

This curious quip about meat resurfaced when I was shooting a scene for the film near the Ponte Vecchio, the "Old Bridge" spanning the Arno River, which winds its way through Florence, Italy. Over a thousand years ago, this bridge was lined with shops of local butchers, who used the bridge for a meat market. After cutting the choice parts from the meat, they threw the leftover, unwanted carcasses into the Arno River below, until the water reeked with the smell of rotting flesh. In 1593, a magistrate named Medici Grand Duke of Tuscany decided to shut down the meat market. Then he reopened the shops to house jewelers and sellers of gold. Today those gold shops are still open, and when they close for the evening, the shop doors are cleverly designed to look like the tops of treasure chests.

Standing on the bridge that day, I realized the Old Bridge carries a deeper story about beauty. It is really our story—yours and mine—and it carries the cure for the world's obsession with perfection. The "meat market" of this world desires to use us

*Sophia Rosenbaum, "Models Keep Getting Skinnier and Skinnier," *New York Post,* June 9, 2016.

and throw us away, quickly tossing us overboard when we can't keep up with the stressful quest for performance and praise. How many times do we end up feeling awkwardly unwanted because we can't meet the expectations of life, others, or even ourselves? It is a battle we can't win! However, there is a King who sees beauty where the world sees none. One word from Him transforms the human heart from a peddler of flesh into a keeper of gold.

Soon after shooting the documentary in Italy, I had an idea. As a freelance filmmaker with a passion for adventure, I felt a

Photo of Rebecca Friedlander in Italy, courtesy of Peter Friedlander.

little quiver of excitement stir in my heart. What if I created a TV series that documented authentic beauty and Christ's transforming work in women around the world? I had no budget and no financial backing, and I knew the series would mean a lot of work. So I did what I normally do when my creative juices start flowing: I started to pray.

"God," I said, making a simple, honest request, "please show me Your plan." Sometimes our Father speaks so unmistakably that even in the bustle of our thoughts and emotions, we recognize His voice as clearly as a sheep knows its shepherd. This was one of those moments.

"This is not just your plan," the Father said. "It's My plan too."

The next day a friend who owned a charity thrift shop called me out of the blue. "Come to our warehouse and pick out whatever you want. I want to give to your ministry." I jumped on her offer!

Dazed, I emerged from her building with armloads of ball gowns and props. A few days later, I crammed my car full of tripods, lenses, makeup, and curling wands and started my first trek from Nashville to the West Coast. Then I called every connection I could dream up and scheduled interviews with dozens of women around the world who had credible stories of transformation and hope. In the end, I styled before-and-after makeover shoots with thirty women in five countries as I followed the quest for true beauty around the world for nine months.

I traveled by air, bus, and motorboat. I lugged my suitcases into subways and up far too many staircases. I even filmed while riding horseback. Once I filmed in a hostel that was right next door to a zoo, and I could hear the peacocks shriek and watch white tigers prowling outside my window! The women came from various backgrounds: the fashion industry, strip clubs, pastors' homes, and families broken and whole. After I filmed the interviews, I turned the footage into a TV show called *Radical Makeovers*, which was broadcast in over a dozen nations and streamed worldwide on international television networks. This book features the best of those stories and shares far more details than included in the show.

The thread running through each makeover is that God is the Author of beautiful stories. In each photo shoot, He was the unseen guest at the table and the delighted Storyteller who was bursting with pride at His daughter's journey toward wholeness. I could sense His tears as each woman related ugly moments of past rejection, and I could sense His smile as she revealed those first moments when the fresh light of true beauty dawned in her journey. I noted that even when we grab the pen and scribble meaningless, blundering paragraphs in our life stories, He patiently waits for us to turn the manuscript over to His nail-scarred hands, which craft the story far better than we can. We discover that the true beauty He has prepared for His daughters is classic—like a timeless string of fine pearls—and once we own it, we carry it our entire lives.

My prayer is that these makeover images and stories will capture your heart and that the keys we discover together will inspire you to unlock the powerful gift of your own value. You are not a piece of flesh at a meat market; you are gold. In a world that demeans and misuses women and beauty, may this book tell the age-old truth in a fresh way: you are loved, you are valued, and you were created to carry true beauty that will never grow old. Together, let's journey around the world on this epic expedition called *Finding Beautiful*.

one

Beautiful Security

The most beautiful people we have known are those who have known defeat, known suffering, known struggle, known loss, and have found their way out of the depths. These persons have an appreciation, a sensitivity, and an understanding of life that fills them with compassion, gentleness, and a deep loving concern. Beautiful people do not just happen.

—*Elisabeth Kübler-Ross*

I lugged my cameras and props over the worn cobblestones in Paris while soft rain pattered on my black umbrella. Several friends helped me carry cardboard, a picture frame, a tripod, and a mirror, and we entered a tiny café on the corner of an enchanting alley. Casual charm in Parisian style caught my eye: the walls were carelessly lined with old books, a fresh strawberry shortcake sat in the window, and the cracking plaster divulged that the City of Love was over a thousand years old. We promptly ordered hot chocolate, which arrived with towering peaks of whipped cream, and began to chat about our photo shoot.

She is tossed by waves but does not sink.

—*official motto of Paris, France, on the national seal*

Our makeover girl was Lucie, a woman in her midtwenties with a cute bob haircut and a mischievous smile, who worked as a team leader at a missionary base in Paris. Her infectious laugh made our conversation easy, and her eyes twinkled with fun and excitement, as if she was determined to radically redefine the term *missionary* for her generation. In fact, Lucie looked as if she could throw a street party at any minute! I wondered what drew this vivacious young woman to Paris and how she chose a life dedicated to sharing the gospel of Christ in the City of Love. As it turned out, Lucie's story resonates with the heartbeat of every woman who longs for safety and true love, and her story holds many secrets for becoming beautifully secure.

Lucie's Story

Tucked away in the iconic countryside of Switzerland, Lucie enjoyed the simple childhood pleasures of being a farmer's daughter. A tomboy, she loved playing in the backyard sandbox with her brothers' toy tractors and was happy to tag along as the only girl behind her three older brothers. Her father was Mennonite and her mother Catholic, so she learned about God's existence at a young age, but He always felt distant and remote—like a faraway force that didn't apply to her. She enjoyed a simple life: the family raised sheep, milked cows, and lived on a secluded farm out of sight from neighbors. Life was peaceful and safe.

School was another matter. On Lucie's first day at the small country classroom, Lucie and her mom both cried as they parted, and life in the new environment felt harsh to the gentle child. Students were unkind and cruel; they mocked her hand-me-down clothes from her brothers, made fun of her French language skills, and said she would never succeed in life. A boy in the desk behind her pulled out a lighter and burned her hair, scorching the ends of her ponytail when the teacher wasn't looking. Lucie dreaded winter, since she had to walk from the school to the bus stop through mounds of snow. Boys from her class would tackle her, stuffing her face, coat, and even inner clothing with snow until she was wet and soaked. It was a prank they regularly played on many children, but Lucie bore the brunt of their torment for years.

Lucie began to have panic attacks at night, terrified of the bullying. Fear filled her mind as her heart began to race, and her throat constricted as she fought to breathe.

I'm dying, she thought as she lay in bed, paralyzed and afraid of death. Repeatedly, her concerned parents wondered if she had a heart problem and took her to the doctor, but no diagnosis was confirmed. The attacks continued, and her social anxiety increased. Shrinking into a shell within herself, Lucie became the insecure, shy girl that no one befriended.

At age sixteen, she moved from the farm to start an apprenticeship at a bakery.

No more will I cower, she inwardly vowed, with her teeth set and chin raised. *I refuse to be that awkward girl anymore.*

With a little makeup, a new hairstyle, and a determination to fake confidence until she made new friends, Lucie started her new job. Nobody knew her in the town, so on her first day of work, she decided to be open, happy, and extroverted. It worked. Everyone loved her, and she was quickly invited to party with new friends and alcohol. This was all new for Lucie, but she decided to willingly try anything to make people accept her. She loved her new persona of being the party girl, but sometimes she wondered if there was more to life than having to "dress up" her emotions every day in order to be loved. Social acceptance was handed to her, but it was an empty glass, and she had to keep performing to fill it. Sometimes the old fears emerged even though she fought so hard to silence them.

One night after drinking alcohol with friends, she smoked an entire pack of cigarettes and arrived back at her apartment just as a panic attack started. Fear leapt at her throat as her heart raced and her body started shaking. *I've smoked too much and my body can't handle it,* she thought in terror, wondering what would happen. Suddenly, everything she had ever heard about God came into her head. Alone in her empty apartment, she shouted, "Jesus! If what I've heard about You is true, come help me! I need You now!"

Instantly, her head cleared and the effects of the alcohol vanished. A strong peace flooded her, calming her racing heart as she sensed the presence of Jesus fill the room. Lucie was shocked by the entrance of her Savior. *Even when I was stuck in a mess of bad choices, He still came to me,* she pondered. She didn't have to do the right thing to be heard by God. In fact, she had been in the middle of an alcohol- and smoke-induced panic attack when she had simply cried out for help. The wonder of God's love crept over her, and for the first time, she felt no anxiety. A strange security was offered to her—something she had never felt before. It wasn't dependent on the safety of her environment or sheltered life but rather met her as she stumbled into the arms of her Savior almost accidentally. This beautiful security caught her completely unaware. Totally at rest, she curled up in her bed still wearing her clothes and fell asleep.

The metamorphosis had begun, and Lucie started believing there was more to life than just being accepted by her peers. Now she began to feel a tug on her heart whenever she started to drink or do something just to please the crowd. The conviction of the Holy Spirit began to prompt her, and she realized a different makeover needed to happen. A hunger stirred for something deeper than an updated appearance and new friends. She had glimpsed a far greater beauty that pierced her heart and gave her a reason to live, so she began to seek out more of God and started attending a local church.

One day the Holy Spirit spoke to her strongly, urging her to attend a discipleship training school in another country so she could learn more about her faith. Torn, Lucie realized that a six-month commitment to this international school would require some hard choices. The quiet safety of her family's farm had been her refuge, stability, and hiding place from the outside world, and she loved returning there for holidays and weekends. She would have to leave it behind if she obeyed. She also had been dating a young man for three years and now realized he was not the best match for her. She would need to

let go of the relationship if she moved forward with Jesus. Even Switzerland, her home country, would be set aside if she followed the prompting. Following Christ meant leaving every security behind and trusting Him to take care of her, but Lucie was determined to cling to her newfound peace in Christ. So she left her family, her job, and her nation and moved to the dorms at her new school. Little did she know that God was removing every security blanket because He was about to make her whole.

To lead the orchestra, you have to turn your back on the crowd.

—Max Lucado

One of the secrets of God's kingdom is that following Christ often leads us to the very thing we were hoping to find all along. Like a caterpillar gazing wistfully at the sky, we have a desire to fly that is embedded in our DNA, but we have neither muscles nor wings to meet the challenge. Only by vulnerably placing ourselves in the hands of our Creator can the metamorphosis reach deeply enough into our souls, until we shed the old skin and soar into the heavens. To prepare us for His new wings, God may require us to sacrifice our old securities, but we discover that He holds the key to our destiny.

At school, Lucie was challenged by her teacher to let God talk to her in a personal way. Awkwardly sitting in silence, she asked God how He would like to speak, and suddenly in her mind's eye she saw a picture of her heavenly Father giving her a lollipop. Lucie loved sweets, and she realized that God knew her heart's desire well enough to give her something fun. Like a good father handing her a favorite candy, God was about to give her a wonderful gift.

God, do You really accept me as I am? she wondered incredulously. *You are so close that You even want to give me a lollipop?*

It was a simple thing, but Lucie realized that the attention and affection she craved were so close. In fact, they were inside her already because Christ was alive in her heart. Her Father in heaven was even nearer than her own heartbeat, and she could access His love and presence whenever she wished. Everything changed as God began to wrap the deepest places of her soul in His embrace. She often slipped away to quiet places to contemplate, admire, and worship God as she listened to worship music and read His Word. In those simple times, the Father began to remove the negative, bullying words that had wormed their way into her soul like greedy parasites, attempting to rob her identity and steal her joy. Truth began to fill those empty places, and she began to believe it: *I am wanted and accepted by the King of Kings and Lord of Lords! He is close to me, and nothing can separate me from His love. I am more than a conqueror through Him who loves me.*

The panic attacks slowly ceased until she was completely healed. Love was her liberty bell, pealing loud and clear in this bright new future in which she was finally secure enough to be herself. God's love met her at the core of her soul, and now she was free to confidently travel, learn new languages, and form healthy friendships.

Today she lives in Paris, France, and serves as the coleader of a mission base that reaches out with love and hope to the city. No longer the shy, insecure girl, Lucie leads mission teams around the world, organizes international events, and shares Christ with complete strangers on the street. Bubbling with joy, this passionate young woman is a rising leader whose confidence comes from truly knowing Christ. In the past, she ran to the family farm for the feeling of safety; today she runs to the arms of her Savior.

"Sometimes I still struggle with fear," she confided, "but I know that my security comes from Christ as I follow His will for my life. Sometimes people speak against me, but it doesn't touch my identity because God's love is so real to me. It's important to spend time in the presence of God, so I take time in His Word to listen to His voice and what He says about me. Knowing Him and knowing who you are empower you to just *be*. That security is truly beautiful."

Photo Shoot

I snapped Lucie's before photos in a back alley in Paris covered in street art. In this area where spray painting is legal, buildings on both sides of the street blaze with color as new artists layer

23

their flamboyant paintings on top of yesterday's designs. I posed Lucie in a hoodie with the sleeves rolled up and wrote on her arms DESPISED and REJECTED. Then I filled her hands with pieces of thick glass and propped the word SHATTERED on top. With the explosion of color at her back, Lucie's photos silently shouted a story of muted pain.

Then I gave Lucie a makeover, and we took the metro (or subway, for my American friends) downtown to the Louvre. After meandering around the buildings, we found a quiet corner to snap some photos. It was drizzling, and I posed Lucie with a black umbrella and called out, "Just have fun! Give me some poses to play with!"

So Lucie jumped in the air holding signs labeled SAFE and CONFIDENT with the joyous freedom of a carefree child. While nearby tourists were stoic and composed, Lucie laughed and twirled as we celebrated the delightful security of belonging to the King of Kings!

My Story

Paris turned out to be unforgettable for me in a personal way, sharing a reminder that my security is in God alone. It all started that morning when I was traveling to France from the south of England by train, bus, plane, and metro. I finally lugged my suitcases a number of blocks to find an iconic red wooden door on the side of a busy Parisian street. Feeling like a secret agent, I typed the number code on a small keypad and swung the heavy door open, then waited on a buzzer response to open a second, thickly paned glass security door to the foyer. At the top of a winding staircase, Lucie graciously opened the door to welcome me. Mission accomplished: I had arrived on location in Paris.

We chatted about various things, and I was in the middle of saying, "So is this neighborhood pretty safe . . ." when a large crash took us both by surprise, followed by loud shouts in the foyer below. Lucie peeked out the door to see two men angrily yelling and the glass security door shattered and lying in hundreds of pieces at their feet. The break-in happened in broad daylight— a surprise act of violence for no apparent reason. Lucie called the police, and we glanced at each other with wide eyes as she chattered in French on the phone and I wondered what kind of escapade I was about to have in the City of Love.

During the middle of the chaos, I slipped into my new bedroom and began to pray. Outside my window, more angry people gathered in the street, defiantly shouting French accusations for some unknown reason. My natural emotions were intimidation and fear, but I knew that God had sent me here on His mission to capture stories and to spread the truth of His love and that I could run to the shelter of my Savior any time. With that confidence, I knew He would protect me and bring peace to my surroundings, so I began to speak the truth of His Word.

> He who dwells in the secret place of the Most High
> Shall abide under the shadow of the Almighty.
> I will say of the Lord, "He is my refuge and my
>   fortress;
> My God, in Him I will trust " (Ps. 91:1–2)

Quoting the ancient psalm aloud, I reminded myself that God is stronger than any challenge. Growing in confidence, I spoke out loud in the empty bedroom and reminded the enemy of my soul that God was in control.

> You shall not be afraid of the terror by night,
> Nor of the arrow that flies by day,

Nor of the pestilence that walks in darkness,
Nor of the destruction that lays waste at noonday.

A thousand may fall at your side,
And ten thousand at your right hand;
But it shall not come near you. (Ps. 91:5–7)

Within a short time, the city street quieted, the police arrived, and the queasy feeling disappeared from my stomach. Fear left, and I was able to rest after a long day of traveling. The beautiful fact was that the security I needed didn't come from perfect surroundings but rather from the God who remains constant regardless of the circumstances. At any point, we can remind ourselves of this truth and cause our fears to bow to His love, even when we are in unfamiliar territory.

The next morning we discovered the reason for the break-in—a hilarious story! A man on the second story had been smoking a cigarette in his apartment and casually launched a mouthful of spit out his window. Sailing over the street below, it promptly landed on the forehead of a man below who happened to be strolling by on the sidewalk. Horrified, the man became outraged and convinced himself that someone had spit on him as a purposeful insult. He managed to get the entry code to our foyer at the pub down the street, smashed the glass security door, and demanded with a loud voice to know who had committed this injustice! Of course, the police arrived, and the apartment manager pressed charges. I never discovered whether the man ever found the accidental spit launcher or not.

We all have instances when life throws us curveballs (or spitballs) and our inner peace is shaken. They crash into our world without notice, and we wince at the surprise attack. But if Christ is our foundation, we have the greatest Friend possible in times of need. Our security need not depend on what is going on around us but rather Who is inside us. We only need to partner with Him and cry out for our Father to make Himself known, place our trust in the God who hears, and find our security in the fact that we are loved and can rest in His care. It is such a comfort to know that we don't have to fight our battles alone because He is on our side.

God's Story (Judg. 6–7)

Cowering behind the house, Gideon did his work secretly, hoping to avoid the eyes of the greedy robbers who stole anything of value. The young man carried shafts of golden wheat behind the old stone winepress and quietly separated the chaff from the kernels of grain, determined to store enough flour to feed his family. Survival was his only goal, since the enemy armies of Midian had trampled the land of Israel and continued to loot the villages, driving Gideon to this undercover act to scrape together enough food to live.

Suddenly, Gideon realized he was not alone, but it was not a rebel soldier who regarded him—it was an angel. The messenger stopped Gideon in his tracks with the greeting, "The Lord is with you, mighty man of valor!"

Astonished, Gideon immediately voiced his bitter thoughts toward the angel. "If the Lord is with us, why have all these terrible things happened to us? Our fathers have told us about His miracles, so where is He today when enemy armies surround us?"

"Go in your strength, and you will save Israel from the Midianites. Haven't I just sent you?"

Gideon's frustration grew, and he began to argue with the angel, venting all his insecurities at once. "How can I save my nation Israel?" he asked incredulously. "My family is poor, and I'm the least significant in status of all my relatives."

Like a father who patiently hears the complaint of his child and gives him that you-still-have-to-obey-me look, God spoke to Gideon. "I will be with you, and you will smite the Midianites, single-handedly overcoming them."

Fear still crippled Gideon, so he asked for a sign to prove that God was really speaking. He made a meal of meat and bread for his guest and placed it on a rock, and when the angel touched his staff to the gift, fire miraculously shot out of the rock and consumed the food. Gideon was terrified! This was the real deal—a personal visit from the Most High. Destiny was knocking on his door.

"I've seen God!" he said, panicked, for during those days, no one could see God and live.

"Be at peace and don't be afraid," the Lord spoke comfortingly. "You will not die."

In response, Gideon built an altar of stones and called it Jehovah Shalom, meaning "The Lord is my peace." He discovered that every time he stepped out and followed the voice of God, amazing things happened that were far beyond his own potential. Gideon even led a group of three hundred soldiers into battle and wiped out an army of thousands, simply because he obeyed the Lord and followed His lead. An entire nation became free because one man embraced God's plan and clung to the security found in the place of obedience.

True Beauty Tip

Often the world defines beauty as self-confidence, but God calls us to follow Him and become Christ confident because His plan for our lives is bigger than what we can accomplish on our own. Like a power cord plugged into a wall outlet, we suddenly come alive when He is our source. Plugged into His Word and presence, we can thrive and be beautifully secure.

Questions for Reflection

1. Are there some ways God has asked you to obey Him in the past, and how have you seen Him come through?
2. Has this built your feeling of security and Christ confidence?
3. Is God asking you to follow Him in any new areas? Explain.
4. What are some of the joys of obeying Christ?

two

Beautiful Daughter

The beauty of a woman must be seen from in her eyes, because that is the doorway to her heart, the place where love resides.
—Audrey Hepburn

Barbed wire wound loosely around a splintered fence post, its rusted ends disappearing into matted grass. No life stirred in the gutted, single-wide trailer that had long ago been abandoned by those who called it home. Camera in hand, I slipped into the front yard with my makeover girl, a slender, soft-spoken muse with long brown hair and large brown eyes. While getting ready for her before photos at this empty trailer, Brittny surveyed the boarded-up ruins.

"This place looks a lot like the house I grew up in," she said quietly as we stood together. "My siblings and I were dubbed 'the river rats in the trailer house' by our peers. We grew so familiar with the smell of liquor and cigarettes at home that we became the butt of cruel jokes at school when we carried the odor everywhere we went."

Tiny yellow flowers pressed through the rubble of the front yard, defying its chaos with beauty. Holding scraps of cardboard, Brittny scrawled words with a black marker to describe the haunting whispers that followed her for many years. With no makeup, tousled hair, and gentle eyes a bit tired from the weight of the memories, she posed in the flowering weeds for photos and held up the words she had chosen: WORTHLESS and TRAILER TRASH.

I looked in Brittny's eyes and saw no lingering shadows from her past. She could stare into the face of the past and confidently call it a liar, knowing without a doubt that she was not defined by that chapter of her story. The love she carried, like the tiny flowers at her feet, refused to be held back from making a persistent entrance into a difficult world. Tenaciously pushing past the debris, it shone brightly for the world to see. *This*, I pondered, *is a victorious tale we all need to hear.*

Brittny's Story

Brittny was a fighter from the first moment she entered the world. Four days after she was born, her mom took her to church, and during the service, the baby began to choke violently. Alarmed, her mother slipped out into the hall and began to pray, commanding any forces of darkness to leave her child.

"Satan, you cannot have Brittny! You are not taking her away from church."

Immediately, the choking ceased, and the infant returned to a peaceful sleep. Her mother's prayers for Brittny's soul were also answered, and Brittny was drawn to God as a young child. However, life at home became difficult as her parents fell into

troubled times. Her father's anger often raged out of control, while her mother began using alcohol to cope with her depression and left the children to clean and keep house. Their trailer began to fall into disrepair, with holes in the floor and piles of dirty dishes that never quite got cleaned. As a child, Brittny was put in charge of cleaning the kitchen, but she couldn't stay on top of it all. Roaches took over the home, and cigarette smoke filled the air, clinging to the children's clothes. At school, they were often bullied because of the smell that stuck to them.

"You're ugly and stupid! You stink!" they jeered, forcing gentle Brittny into a corner with the other social outcasts, who banded together for survival. They weren't friends by choice but because there was no one left. The stinging words from her peers were seared into her thoughts, leaving a deep hurt behind as the social shunning continued. From second to eighth grade, Brittny struggled with undiagnosed depression.

Tears became a frequent medication for her fragile soul, and she would often melt into tearful bewilderment when life felt hard. Mirroring her trembling heart, her pale face would sometimes cloud with pain as the tears flowed. One day her father saw her crying and, thinking that her weeping was a sign of weakness, spoke the words that labeled her for years. "You're worthless!" he declared with annoyance, embarrassed by her tears.

Stunned, Brittny heard nothing else. The words echoed like a shout in a vacant hallway, bouncing back and forth until they filled every empty space. Longing to run into the arms of a father who could offer her comfort, she was met with anger instead. The word *worthless* was the label she wore for many years, ducking her head in shy surrender to its constant voice. She knew her dad loved her, but he constantly hammered her self-worth like an anvil, shaping the soft tissue of her heart with belittlement instead of trust. The tears continued in secret places where she hoped no one would see, and the terror of God began to seep into her soul.

If God is my Father, what if He thinks I'm worthless? Brittny wondered in private. *Everyone says that God loves me, but I know my dad loves me, and yet he still hurts me deeply. Is God the same way?* She loved Jesus and would often talk to Him in childlike delight, but the figure of God the Father filled her mind with dread. What if she did something wrong—would He strike her dead in anger? Did He misunderstand her and have no interest in her life? And what about other men in her world—did they think she was worthless too?

In high school, Brittny was asked on dates by several guys, but they were not people she wanted to go out with, so she turned them down. One day while she sat alone in the cafeteria, the chatter of teenage voices faded into the background as she heard the quiet voice of Christ speak to her heart. "Look around the room at the students and watch their relationships."

Scanning the interactions of her classmates, she recognized the cycle she knew all too well: the cat-and-mouse chase of dating and breaking up that left a chaotic trail of heartbreak. Brittny was annoyed with her high school friends who kept returning to this vicious cycle. Rolling her eyes, she would often tell them to quit being stupid and hurting themselves as they jumped from relationship to relationship.

"Now look at My face," the gentle voice whispered with a tender invitation.

Brittny closed her eyes and imagined the face of Jesus. To her surprise, the picture that came to her mind's eye was the face of Christ with tears running down His cheeks in deep compassion. He was not berating her peers; rather, He felt the pain of their broken relationships, and His own heart was hurting. Brittny was shocked as she saw the love of her heavenly Father clearly for the first time in the image of a weeping father. In the same way a good parent runs to a child who is hurting and even cries himself when feeling their pain, God weeps when we weep.

I never realized, thought Brittny in awe, *that when God gave His Son for us, we became a part of Him, just like Christ is a part of the Father. He doesn't despise my tears. In fact, He cries with me.*

Coming face-to-face with the Father's love began to slowly shift Brittny's thinking: God the Father wanted her to be safe, and even if her earthly father was not there to coach her through life, her heavenly Father was there to help her navigate high school relationships.

"My God," she prayed, "if these constant, hurtful relationships are so heartbreaking to You, what should I do?"

Tenderly, she heard the voice of her Father say, "Don't date."

"Don't go out with anyone?" she responded incredulously. "How am I going to meet the right man?"

"I will show you," the voice responded to her fears.

After that cafeteria prayer, Brittny made the conscious choice to wait for God's man in her life. Any time a guy asked her out, she boldly told him the story of how God told her to wait for the right man, and each time the suitor quickly made a beeline for the exit. Somehow that didn't bother Brittny, because she knew that her Father God had a plan.

Fashion is not necessarily about labels. It's not about brands. It's about something else that comes from within you.

—Ralph Lauren

For several years, she simply waited until, at the age of eighteen, a young man entered her world. Jason loved Jesus with all his heart, and when he heard Brittny's story of how she was waiting on God, it made him love her even more than he had already begun to. They became best friends, praying together, reading God's Word, and talking all the time. She realized that he was just right for her, and they got married two years later.

Although her faith in God was strong, Brittny's personal confidence was still shattered. When Jason would tell her how beautiful she was, she would shrug her shoulders and flippantly say, "Whatever!"

The words "You're worthless, ugly, and stupid, and you stink" still stuck fast like daggers in her heart, and she thought Jason's compliments were made out of obligation. One day he stopped her in the middle of her rebuff and countered, "You are not going to say whatever anymore! You are going to say thank you."

Brittny rolled her eyes and complied with a laugh. However, the more she began to thank people for their sincere compliments, the more she started hearing their words of affirmation echo back in her head instead of the lies. With a simple thank-you, she welcomed the new, affirming words into her heart, and they began to blot out the lies. Over time, Jason's love began to speak louder than the lies of her past, and she could look in the mirror and actually believe she was a beautiful, worthy woman of God. Today Brittny is a mom of two children, and parenting has given her an even greater perspective on God's love. Even through the challenges of guiding toddlers, she recognizes that the unconditional love she has for her children is how God loves us.

"No matter what my kids have done, my love doesn't change," she confided. "When my child gets hurt, my first instinct is to run to help them, even if it hurts me in the process. Our Father God's love is the same: Christ went to the cross to show us that He would pay the greatest price to save us. Our God is a good Father who wants the best for us too."

Photo Shoot

I captured Brittny's before shots at the abandoned trailer, with its broken windows and sagging floorboards, as she held the signs labeled WORTHLESS and TRAILER TRASH. I was glad to finish that shoot and leave the site. Brittny was a champ, but I knew she didn't belong there, and placing such a dreary backdrop behind her beautiful face was difficult for me. We left the neglected property and tore up her ragged cardboard sign into tiny bits as we drove away.

For Brittny's after photos, I decided that our Cinderella needed a new wardrobe. My fairy godmother powers might come through a curling wand instead of a magic one, but I use what I have. I wound her long hair into soft waves that flowed down her back. Then I dressed her in a golden gown of beaded silk that flared at the waist. With strings of pearls around her neck and soft makeup with mauve tones, she looked like a fairy princess. I draped a dozen elegant, pink roses over her arm to finish the look, and we drove to one of my favorite locations: an old, European-style mansion with sweeping stone fences and glorious arches. Towering trees bent gracefully over a stone gazebo and manicured yard, creating a dreamy castle tucked away in the historical neighborhood. As Brittny stepped from her carriage (aka my trusty white Toyota), I gave her a mirror and a marker to document the new look.

"Okay, Brittny," I said, "give me some words to describe the place Jesus has brought you to today. What words define you now?"

With a huge smile on her face, Brittny wrote WORTHY, LOVED, and BEAUTIFUL. Framed with gold, the mirror told the new story of this woman who sees herself as the daughter God calls her to be. This is not an identity she conjures up by herself; it is how her heavenly Father sees her, and she simply embraces His personal delight in His child. Our Father loves to remind us that we are His beautiful daughters.

My Story

Sometimes we need a sweet moment with our Father so He can tell us how much He adores us. One day I asked Him for reassurance of His care, and I was amazed by the response.

I was working in a Christian ministry and spending long hours in discipleship and prayer. I loved watching the transformation that can happen in people's lives, but let's face it: ministry is a lot of work and sometimes feels like living at summer camp all year long. Emotionally, I felt depleted, and one day I had a quiet conversation with God.

"Father," I prayed, "I believe that You love me because Your Word tells me so, but would You show me in a tangible way? Would You send one of Your people to remind me of that love?"

That week I was invited to the campus of a missionary training center, and I joined a friend for breakfast at one of the private homes. We made small talk and chatted for a bit, then I thanked the hosts for the meal, hugged my friend, and left. Afterward, I decided to pay a quick visit to one of my favorite spots on the campus: a tiny chapel with an old spinet piano in the corner. The building was empty as I entered and slid behind the yellowed keys, ready to enjoy a quiet moment of worship. Suddenly, the door opened and in walked the missionary who had just hosted me for breakfast in her home. She was a little embarrassed and tried hard to be polite.

"I was about to drive to town," she began, "when the Holy Spirit stopped me. 'I want you to give Rebecca a gift,' He said. I was surprised, because I just met you today, and it didn't seem fitting to give a gift to someone I don't know well. 'What do you want me to give her?' I asked awkwardly. 'The pearls from China,' He said. 'But, Lord,' I protested, 'that's the kind of gift that a gentleman might give a lady. I don't want her to get the wrong impression from me! However, I'll do it if You want me to.'"

Almost apologetically, the woman held out a little golden bag while I sat at the piano fighting tears of amazement. To my astonishment, inside the pouch was a pearl necklace and stud earrings. I knew beyond a shadow of a doubt that God had heard my prayer request for a tangible gift of love, and my Daddy was giving His daughter a gift through the hands of this generous missionary.

"It might sound funny to you," I said through a blur of tears, "but I know exactly why God told you to give me these pearls. Thank you for your obedience."

I sat at the piano, and brand-new words flowed as I poured out my heart to my Father:

> You call me loved
> When I am lonely
> You call me close
> When I'm afraid of the dark
> You call me home
> When I go running
> And You say, Child,
> Come run into My arms again
>
> And I call, Daddy, Daddy, come and hold me
> Like only, only You can
> I call, Daddy, Daddy, come and love me
> Like only You can
>
> You call me beautiful
> Though I may argue with the mirror
> You call me precious
> You say that I have nothing to fear
> You call me Yours
> You call me worth dying for

And I can't run from a love
That's just too hard to ignore

Ever since that moment, I have been overwhelmed by the thought of how deeply our Father cares for His children. No deed goes unnoticed, no prayer is too small, and no wish to know His love goes unheeded. He is such a kind Father, and it is an incredible joy to be His daughter.

God's Story (Isa. 64:8; Ps. 27:10; Rom. 8:15)

When it comes to perceiving God as our Father, many of us have difficulty viewing Him through this lens because of tragic circumstances surrounding our earthly fathers. The very word *father* is powerful enough to conjure up emotions of either joy or grief. Sometimes we need to turn to a fresh page and allow our Father in heaven to define Himself based on accurate descriptions in Scripture rather than defining Him based on what our past or society tells us. I have worn a path in my Bible from flipping to some of these verses, and they provide keys to reexamine the heart of our Father God. Here are a few of my favorites:

> But now, O Lord,
> You are our Father;
> We are the clay, and You our potter;
> And all we are the work of Your hand. (Isa. 64:8)

This verse speaks of the beauty of God's role as a Father. We are created by God. Each of us was "created" by a father and a mother, so the verse doesn't sound too profound until we look at the second part of the verse: we are clay, and He is the potter. No potter creates a vessel haphazardly but rather uses incredible thought, precision, and care to shape a vessel from a lump of clay. The potter delights in the result and is proud of their creation. Our Father God didn't make us as an afterthought; He deliberately formed us like an artist creating a masterpiece on the wheel. God deliberately made us and takes pride in His work because that is the kind of Father He is.

> When my father and my mother forsake me,
> Then the Lord will take care of me. (Ps. 27:10)

In Hebrew, the phrase "take care of me" is a single word meaning "to gather." Our Father God promises that, if for any reason our fathers and mothers are unavailable to meet our needs, He will gather us to Himself. As in the case of Brittny, perhaps our parents were or are emotionally unavailable. Nevertheless, God is such a good Father that He finds ways of stepping in when we need Him most, even when our family members don't measure up to what they need to be, because His heart for us is so huge.

> For you did not receive the spirit of bondage again to fear, but you received the Spirit of adoption by whom we cry out, "Abba, Father." (Rom. 8:15)

Some of the greatest parents I know are heroes because they have chosen to adopt children. I am awed by the hearts of these men and women who delight in sharing their homes with children they have no obligation to help. God is this kind of Father. His heart overflows with so much love that He wants to gather us all into His home, if we will just let Him, because His heart is that big.

This verse also reminds us that we don't have to be stiff and stoic with God, because He has placed His Spirit inside all true believers. It is that Spirit, like a little piece of Himself, who cries out, "Daddy God, I love you!" He loves when His children desire an active relationship with Him, because He wants that too.

43

These verses remind us that God is truly our Father and that He is more deeply in love with His daughters than we can even imagine.

True Beauty Tip

Learning to experience God as our Father enables us to receive our identity as women of God. Embracing His joy, tears, and companionship is a powerful key to unlocking beauty in our everyday lives.

Questions for Reflection

1. What are a few words that describe your relationship to your earthly father?
2. Have you felt known and cherished in a healthy way by your earthly father?
3. How does God's Word describe your heavenly Father?
4. God's Word says that you are intimately known by the Father. Does this empower you? Explain.

three

Beautiful Adventure

Never lose an opportunity of seeing anything that is beautiful; for beauty is God's handwriting—a wayside sacrament.
—*Ralph Waldo Emerson*

When we think of adventurous women throughout history, names such as Amelia Earhart, Harriet Tubman, and Joan of Arc come to mind. Every once in a while we meet a young woman who reminds us that passionate leaps of faith can still happen today. I filmed a makeover shoot with one of these adventurers, and doing so required a wilderness expedition.

"I always keep an adventure kit in my car," Lauren confided, her brown eyes dancing as we rounded a steep bend shadowed by the eastern Sierras. "In the winter, I pack skis, a sled, gloves, and chains for my tires. If adventure calls, I want to be ready!"

I listened with delight, observing the stunning scenery as we drove near a ski resort town just north of Yosemite, California.

Each new curve in the road presented new vistas of white-capped mountains, and Lauren fit so easily into all this beauty. I watched her fearlessly climb a steep hill with a sled over her shoulder just for the thrill of whizzing down a moment later. Still, it was hard to believe Lauren had traveled around the world alone, and the more I heard of her story, the more intrigued I became. Her passport stamped by dozens of countries, Lauren prompted curious questions. How did this darling young woman become a world traveler before the age of thirty? Was she running away or chasing after something?

We arrived at a cozy lodge at the foot of the mountains and brewed a cup of tea. Then with her slender figure curled into a comfy chair, Lauren unfolded her inspiring tale. She reminds us that a rewarding adventure may be waiting just around the corner.

Lauren's Story

Lauren was perfect—at least that is what everyone told her. With the figure of a model, a smart mind that helped her excel in school, and high standards among her peers, she had everything going for her. Her pastor called her the Mother Teresa poster child for her youth group because she didn't drink or smoke and honestly tried to show compassion for others. Yet beneath the surface, Lauren knew this good girl wasn't perfect. In fact, an embarrassing whisper ran through her head, questioning whether she could live up to the high expectations placed on her. The weight of being the "perfect Christian" was a daunting load to carry, so she bit her lip and wondered, *Can I keep everyone happy?* Lifting her chin, she determined to keep smiling and perform as best she could.

Plowing through high school, Lauren planned to attend a good college, study graphic design, and live the American dream in hopes of being a positive example for Christ in the business world. Surely, if God was looking for role models to shine brightly for Him, Lauren was the choice for Christian achievement. Yet looking back, Lauren realizes that her momentum was fueled more by the desire to please people than by the desire to please Jesus, but at the time, she was everyone's Christian superstar.

One ordinary day, as she was walking through her high school, God asked Lauren a question in His still, small voice that rocked her world. "Lauren, what if I asked you to do something different with your life?"

Nervously, Lauren wondered what God was asking of her. As she recalled a recent opportunity presented to her youth group, the thought crossed her mind, *What if God is calling me to take a mission trip?* She decided to take a chance and step out of her comfortable world, so at sixteen years of age, she joined a team traveling to India for relief work.

Life was far from neat and tidy in India. In a third-world hospital, she was shocked to see rows of beds filled with amputees and leprosy patients. With wide eyes and tentative steps, she followed her team through a vortex of halls and corridors, catching sight of one isolated bed covered with mosquito netting. Inside, a slender woman about twenty years old lay on the sheets—her body covered with terrible burns. A strange blend of empathy and curiosity welled up in Lauren, and she asked the hospital attendant what had happened to the patient.

"She set herself on fire," the attendant responded, refusing to supply any further information. Looking into the numb, unresponsive eyes of the girl, Lauren felt a pit in her stomach as the thought pierced her, *They're not telling the truth. No young woman in her right mind would intentionally set fire to her body.* Later she learned the ugly story of this girl's probable fate.

The Indian women told her that bride burning is an ancient tradition that still happens in their nation. According to some cultures, a bride becomes the personal property of her husband and his family after an arranged marriage. If the dowry isn't paid or the family is not pleased with the woman, they may become angry and see her as a burdensome extra mouth to feed. The family may even douse the girl with kerosene and set her on fire, burning her to death. Every year the Indian police receive thousands of reports of bride burning, and if proven, they are treated as homicides. The woman Lauren saw in the hospital bed was probably a victim of bride burning with no one to plead her cause, so doctors had placed her in a ward and simply claimed she set herself on fire.

The image of the burned woman seared itself in Lauren's mind, and a throbbing compassion beat like a steady drum in her chest. Strumming her guitar, she penned the words to vocalize this new heartbeat:

> Walked into her room that day
> Never knowing that I would be so changed
> Her body burnt from her head down to her toes
> Oh, she did it to herself—so the story goes
> But there's another story that's yet to be told
>
> Won't somebody hear her cry
> Won't somebody hear her side
> There's two sides to every tale
> Won't somebody lend an ear

After Lauren returned to the States, the shock of this scene made her dreams look small, and she began to fall out of love with normal life. No longer thinking about herself and how to impress others with her achievements, Lauren felt the seed of a dream begin to swell in her heart. Somehow she wanted to touch the world with Christ's love. She wanted to hold the forgotten, lonely ones and give them hope, but she felt so helplessly small in a world of overwhelming pain. What could she do?

Over time, the sights and sounds of India began to fade like a dream of another world. Lauren slowly retreated to the everyday life of an American teenager as she buried the dream deep inside. However, God was not going to waste the compassion that had been awakened. During her personal quiet time, God's familiar tug on Lauren's heart came again. "Lauren, will you follow Me? I have more for you."

20 years from now you will be more disappointed by the things that you didn't do than by the ones you did do. So throw off the bowlines. Sail away from the safe harbor. Catch the trade winds in your sails. Explore. Dream. Discover.

—Mark Twain

Lauren lifted her eyes to heaven and took a big breath, realizing that God's plans were exceeding hers by leaps and bounds, so she decided to follow the footsteps of Christ Jesus and say yes to living a life of compassion. After high school, she entered a missionary program and eventually finished a college degree on the mission field. Each time Lauren said yes to God, she found herself jumping on a plane to another country, and the divine mandate of Christ to go into all the world and preach the gospel started to change her perception of Christianity. Her pulse quickened in wonder as she realized that God wasn't looking for perfect people— just people willing to follow Him. Shedding her quest for performance and praise, Lauren shifted into high gear as her life as a modern missionary began. One day she brainstormed like never before.

What would it look like to get an open-ended ticket for a trip around the world, believing that God would provide and open doors for me to love people? she dared to wonder. She would be doing exactly what the first apostles did in the early church. They didn't always have a plan—they just shared the hope of Christ wherever they went.

Lying awake in bed that night, Lauren excitedly traced a map in her head of where her travels might lead. Over the next three

months, she often woke up with the name of a country to visit on her heart—and some of the nations she didn't even know existed! Eventually, she embarked on a yearlong, worldwide trip, simply believing that God would open doors for her to pour compassion on others. This radical plunge into the unknown turned into a wild ride

Singapore, England, Uganda, Morocco, Spain, Thailand, China, South Korea—Lauren simply packed her bags, and the way opened in front of her. Sometimes she had no idea what the purpose of her visit was until she landed in the country, and other times she joined forces with mission teams that were already working on the ground. In Swaziland, where nearly an entire generation had been lost to HIV and AIDS, she wrapped her arms around orphans, distributed donated clothes, and played soccer with abandoned children. In Uganda, she helped women create jewelry to earn a living as they recovered from a life impacted by sex trafficking. In Morocco, she assisted a Christian school by simply being an extra pair of hands for the busy teachers. Repeatedly, Lauren found opportunities to share the hope of Christ, and people embraced her gift. One woman hugged her with deep gratefulness and whispered, "God sent you across the world just for me!"

Lauren realized that God was using this adventure to shape her world too. Christianity wasn't about being perfect. Rather, it was about being available to love others in the name of Jesus and saying yes to following His lead.

Today Lauren lives in a ski resort town outside Yosemite National Park in California, where the eastern Sierras provide both outdoor adventures and a quiet place to reflect. She is working on a book about her life on the road and is enjoying this season at home to bond with her church and community.

"Now I have a real job," she said with a laugh, "and God is teaching me that there is beauty to be found in simple things. Adventuring with God doesn't always require a trip around the world, because the real excitement is discovering people right in front of us who need love. Life is about giving hope to others, and there are so many ways to do that. It may require stepping out of our comfort zone in order to extend a helping hand, but saying yes to God is always a thrill, whether you're reaching across the street or around the world."

Photo Shoot

Layers of snow flanked the mountain road as we parked in front of a tiny country church. For her before photos, I handed Lauren some torn pieces of cardboard and a marker. She wrote on them PERFECTIONIST, PEOPLE-PLEASER, and BOXED IN.

For her after shoot, I styled Lauren in a heavy satin dress and a thick fur coat, and we shot against snowy peaks at sunset. Laughing at the sheer silliness of wearing a big dress in the wilderness, she threw a handful of snow in the air, enjoying the world with wild grace and delight.

I watched Lauren that afternoon, the "perfect" girl frolicking in the winter snow, and thought about how desperately we need to tune in to Jesus's call in our lives. He has created so much beauty for us to enjoy, so many paths for us to follow, and all the tools we need to love a broken world, and yet often we stay in our comfort zone and try to impress Him with our good works and fancy deeds. Maybe we have quashed our longing for beauty

and adventure, trying to mute its demand to be heard by calling it "unreasonable" and "irresponsible." Yet could it be that our longing is our own heart crying for a deeper, more radical faith? Dare we believe that our Father could tenderly call to us, as He did to Lauren, "Child, will you follow Me? I have more for you."

My Story

Sometimes a crazy yes is needed to follow God into His plans for our lives. When I first picked up a camera and started filming, I had no clue what I was doing. Truthfully, I had never wanted to produce videos. I just wanted to write songs and speak in front of audiences. However, I needed someone to produce a DVD for my ministry, and after praying in vain for two years that God would send someone to help, I wondered if I was asking for the wrong thing. So instead, I started praying for a camera and asked my Bible study small group to pray as well. The next day a woman walked into the office where I worked.

"Actually," she said, after hearing of my prayer, "God already told me to buy a camera and donate it to your workplace. Let's get one right now!"

Flabbergasted, I jumped into her car, and we bought the camera I used to make my first ministry film. A year later, God led me to start a TV show on a local cable channel. Though I had no schooling or training in film, through simple, gritty passion and hard work, my little TV show slowly started gaining traction in my local area. After five years, a national Christian network picked up my show, and I have been filming around the world ever since.

God was simply looking for someone to say yes. He could have found someone skilled and educated in broadcasting, and my show would have started off much cleaner and more professional. He could have chosen someone with a great deal of money and big investors or someone who didn't have to hang a green screen in their living room or buy cheap thrift store furniture for a film set, but He didn't. He asked a young woman to do the impossible, and then He helped her do it. I didn't have much to offer, but I said yes, and that is all He needed. Adventures are pretty simple when we go with Jesus.

God's Story (Luke 5:1–11)

Simon Peter, a rugged fisherman with a tough, sun-bronzed face, was washing his nets by the Sea of Galilee. It was a daily, routine chore, and he had no idea his life was about to radically change. While he was minding his own business, a preacher named Jesus from the nearby town of Nazareth walked up and asked to borrow his fishing boat as a platform to preach. Peter shrugged and obligingly let the young man speak to the gathering crowd from the deck of his boat. Afterward, Jesus told Peter, "Launch out into the deep water and lower your nets for a catch."

Knowing that the fish swam only in shallow waters, Peter defensively shot back, "Master, we've worked all night and haven't caught a thing!" Then he caught himself and thought, *What harm could it do? I'll humor the preacher.* "At your word," he said, "I will let down the nets."

Peter threw his nets into the depth of the sea, and suddenly the drifting cords sputtered to life. Hundreds of fish, their silver fins slapping the water in a frenzy, filled the nets. The boat became so full of fish that it began to sink! Peter shouted with both joy and alarm, "James! John!" He roared to his fishing partners, "Get over here and help me! There's more than I can hold!"

Dripping from sweat and spray, Peter realized he was standing in the middle of a miracle. *We fished all night without a bite, but when Jesus spoke, everything changed.* Trembling, he fell down before Jesus and cried, "Leave me alone, Lord! I'm a sinful man!"

Jesus clasped His warm hand on Peter's shoulder and responded, "Don't be afraid. From now on you will catch men."

Stunned by this call, Peter left everything to follow Jesus that day and found himself wrapped in an adventure that overshadowed anything he could have imagined.

∞

Like Peter, we may struggle with insecurity and fear when it comes to following Christ's call, but we can find incredible joy as we say yes to both big and small things. Ultimately, God may not call you into a life of world travel and missions as He did Lauren and the apostle Peter. Maybe your mission field is your hometown. Maybe your assignment is the monumental task of raising a family with integrity and God's love. Each calling presents powerful opportunities to love and serve Christ and to be the hands and feet of Jesus, and each also has its own challenges to overcome with the help of Christ. Maybe our adventure is simply to invite Him to partner with us in a deeper way no matter the place, to exit our comfort zone and dream big dreams of how to share His love.

The real question is this: Are you willing to say yes? Are you willing to follow Him into the unknown, believing that He is faithful? Perhaps it is time to fall out of love with old ideas and lock gazes with the Creator of true adventure. It is time to start dreaming bigger, praying for greater vision, and listening for His voice. He calls to His bride, "Come away with Me. Live for something bigger than yourself. Let Me surprise you." Beautiful adventures await. Will you listen for His call?

True Beauty Tip

A little adventure can add a fresh spark to our lives. Taking a walk in the park while we pray, reaching out to someone in need, or taking a mission trip can add beauty to our world and help our faith grow. Jesus loves adventure and invites us to partner with Him.

Questions for Reflection

1. Does the idea of radical faith excite or intimidate you? Why?
2. If you could do anything in your life for Christ, what would it be?
3. What goal would require stepping out in faith for you to accomplish it?
4. Is God asking you to say yes to Him today in any new ways?

four

Beautiful Already

Let God have you, and let God love you—and don't be surprised if your heart begins to hear music you've never heard, and your feet learn to dance as never before.

—*Max Lucado*

Volcanic mountains lined the road like vaulted cathedrals draped with tropical forests. As I drove my rental car toward the heart of the Hawaiian island of Oahu, thin ribbons of cloud hung over the tree line and parted for a momentary rainbow to span the road. An epic paradise, this island is the prime location for bronzed surfers and fun tourist stops, but I wanted to go a bit deeper and discover stories of the women who live there.

"We don't hang out at Waikiki Beach," the locals told me. "It's a fun destination the first time you visit, but there is so much more to see here."

So steering away from Honolulu, I followed my GPS to meet a young woman named Karla, an island resident with a quick smile and a bubbly personality. We decided to unpack her story on a secluded beach, where an old stone wall held back the waves and huge mountains towered behind us. Perched on the rocks with the ocean breeze at her back, Karla shared her story—a tale of tragedy and triumph that dares us to fully be ourselves.

Karla's Story

The Hawaiian greeting *aloha* means "love, peace, and compassion." It has been said that a true life of *aloha* is when the heart completely overflows with goodness and the bearer gains the ability to influence others with their spirit. Karla's family lived out the true meaning of this word, and her parents pastored a church that constantly shared love with the community. They worked hard to build both the church and their family, and Karla loved the sand, surf, and bright sunshine of Oahu.

At first glance, this Hawaiian girl seemed to have everything going for her, but island life had a dark side: Karla was only seven years old when she was sexually molested by her babysitter, the older sister of her best friend from church. Suddenly, she was uncomfortable at her parents' church and with the atmosphere of high standards and purity. She felt dirty—like something was wrong with her—and even though the abuse was not her fault, it marked her with a big, black scar. Shame sealed her lips, and she was terrified to tell her parents what had happened, certain that it would dishonor their leadership position in the community and they would choose to reject her. *They are so holy*, she reasoned, *but I am not. If I tell them what happened to me, they will despise me forever.*

Locking herself in her room, she shut the painful emotions inside and slipped into rage by playing depressing music and imagining she was the only one in the world with these problems. The pressure of being a pastor's daughter weighed heavily on her, and she was reminded of the standards required to honor her parents and the church. Ashamed of feeling so dirty, she realized she could never measure up to the holiness expected of her. A thick wall grew around her heart, hiding it from the world and those who loved her, and although she secretly desired to follow God, the shame convinced her it was impossible. *I want to be a Christian*, she thought, *but I will never be good enough for that.*

During her teen years, image was everything. With elaborate hair and makeup every day, she set out to create a new image that would capture the attention of her peers. Social media was her getaway—the place she could create the life she wanted to

The public wanted a fairy princess to come and touch them and everything would turn to gold. Little did they realize that the individual is crucifying herself inside because she didn't think she was good enough.

—Princess Diana

have and no one could actually know who she really was. It made her feel like the master of her own destiny; she could be the heroine of her own story and receive the attention she craved. Privately, her heart still cowered in shame and confusion, but on social media, she could paint the picture of the perfect world: freedom, beauty, and life on the beach.

Guys started asking her out, drawn to the sexy girl on social media. Unfortunately, the world she created had monsters inside, and the attention of men came with a terrible price. One date with a surfer on a world-famous Hawaiian beach ended with Karla being completely taken advantage of, and she was crushed, feeling she had lost everything of value. Her perfect virtual world crumbled, and she struggled to keep up the persona, throwing herself into doing everything in her power to be thin. An eating disorder, smoking, and drugs were all part of the package. The girl behind the photos was falling apart, and she still had no idea who she really was.

She began purging after she ate, refusing to keep down food for fear of gaining weight. Eventually, her body started rejecting food whether she made herself vomit or not. Karla's mom took her to doctors and psychologists, but no one seemed to have the magic cure for bulimia, the illness that dominated her life. Her throat was raw from vomiting, and when she started coughing up blood in her early twenties, Karla knew she was in serious trouble. Her pain kept resurfacing to crack her thin disguise, and one day her friend said, "You're not even fun anymore. Why are you so sad all the time? Something must be wrong with you!"

Stunned, Karla realized that she hadn't fixed anything. She had the boyfriend, the looks, and the popularity, so why was she still so sad? During the middle of a late-night party, she called her mom and asked for a ride home. Smelling like alcohol, she tumbled into the family car. *I know I'm not behaving like a good pastor's daughter*, she thought, bracing herself for a lecture. But instead of berating her, Karla's mom turned to her with tears streaming down her cheeks and said, "Karla, I love you. Nothing will make me stop loving you because you're my daughter."

Karla couldn't believe she was hearing correctly. *Why is she being so kind to me?* she wondered in a daze. *Tomorrow is Sunday. I'll go to church with her just because she was nice to me tonight.*

The next morning Karla was hung over from the night before as she slipped into church, but soon she stepped into a curious encounter with God. The sounds of the worship band and congregational singing were muted, as if someone had placed earmuffs on her head. A warm presence came over her and wrapped around her frozen heart. She knew this was God and that He loved her. She didn't feel criticized or condemned by Him, only wrapped in a pureness and light that completely overruled every fear. In a flash, all the effects of her hangover vanished, and she was completely sober. *I feel so good*, Karla thought, *and I should have a splitting headache!* She couldn't quite understand what was happening until the voice of Jesus spoke straight to her heart: "Are you done running yet?"

Karla sat bolt upright, stunned by this encounter. God had met her with His love and embraced her heart, even when she despised herself the most. She jumped from her chair and ran to the front of the church, screaming, "God, I give my life to You! You're real!" Instantly, the members of the congregation swarmed around Karla like a flock of birds. They prayed, hugged her, and enveloped her in so much love that she felt a little embarrassed. On her knees before the altar, Karla listened as the kind voice of Jesus spoke once more to her heart. "I'm already in you," He said, "but don't pretend to serve Me if you can't let go of the idols in your life."

Karla stopped short, realizing that the things she had been turning to for love in the past were idols when compared to the real, powerful love that God offers. Merriam-Webster's dictionary defines an idol as "a representation or symbol of an object of worship; broadly: a false god; a false conception: fallacy; a form or appearance visible but without substance."*

She had hoped to find fulfillment by creating an image on social media, but God was telling her that He loved *her*—not the make-believe image she had worked so hard to fabricate. Drugs and alcohol numbed the pain, but God was challenging her to let go of those crutches and let Him be her Healer. In her desperation to flee the church and the shame of not being good enough, Karla had created her own world, but God wanted to remove the shame and bring her back to the church, where she was called to be. She realized that her way of life was never going to bring her true love. She deleted her social media page, broke up with her boyfriend, and left her job at a highly acclaimed restaurant with a questionable atmosphere.

> *If they don't like you for being yourself, be yourself even more.*
>
> —Taylor Swift

Some of the results were immediate. That day at the altar, her drug and alcohol addictions were miraculously taken away. Never again did she struggle with the urge to drink or misuse substances. Learning to love God again came easily, since she was immediately captivated by the presence of Jesus, but learning to love herself was harder. Karla had hated her body for so many years, and because she was gaining weight and becoming a healthy size, she felt larger than she was used to. Wincing, she struggled with the way her body looked. Some days the frustration was unbearable, and she would bury her head in her pillow,

---

* *Merriam-Webster*, s.v. "idol (*n.*)," accessed September 27, 2018, https:// www.merriam-webster.com/dictionary/idol.

screaming, "God! You have to help me! I don't know how to love myself."

One day she locked herself in her room, picked up a marker, stood in front of the mirror naked, and began to write words on the body parts she didn't like: BEAUTIFUL, FORGIVEN, LOVED. She began to speak blessings over her body parts and call them lovely. "Stomach," she told herself, "I'm sorry for treating you badly. Thank you for holding down my food. There is nothing wrong with you. Legs, you're not fat. I'm so thankful that I have legs when some people do not."

Every day for a month, she wrote and spoke truth over her body, and slowly her vision began to change. At the end of thirty days, she could honestly look at herself and say, "Wow, I'm beautiful. God did a really good job when He made me."

This mind-set makeover brought so much healing that she was actually comfortable in her own skin again. A new confidence began to grow in her heart, and she began to believe that God actually wanted her—mess and all.

"I always felt like I could give Jesus the good, clean parts of my heart," she confided, "but I couldn't give Him the parts that were bleeding, because they were too messy. Then God asked me to let Him take the bandages off. He didn't hate those wounds, and He didn't condemn me. He just said, 'I understand. I know it wasn't your fault. Let Me love you in those places.' It was His perfect love that healed the anxiety in my heart."

Today Karla is finishing Bible school with a degree in pastoral ministry, and she leads the youth group at her church in Oahu, Hawaii. Through her work alongside her parents, she has helped the church become a safe place for other young people to find hope and healing. A young powerhouse preacher, she loves to plant God's Word into the hearts of youth and help them become healed and whole. She says that staying emotionally and physically healthy is still a conscious choice for her, but she has become strong in her resolutions.

"I wake up in the morning and say, 'God, I choose to love myself because You love me. I choose to love others because You love them too.' I can win this fight because He is in me!"

Karla learned to love herself, not because she is perfect but because she fell in love with her Savior and chose to believe what He said about her. As she embraced her position as a woman of God, the true meaning of *aloha* came alive and overflowed her heart with love, peace, and compassion for others. She is unstoppable in her passion to give away the love she has found.

Photo Shoot

For her before photos, Karla and I drove to a gutted cement building covered with flamboyant graffiti. It was littered with trash, and the colorful cinder block walls housed only piles of refuse and rusted scraps of metal. Posing in front of huge, colorful art, she stood like a lost child in the midst of a war of words, and her scraps of cardboard carried the labels ABANDONED, REJEC-TION, and UGLY.

The after photo shoot location required an adventurous hike. I curled Karla's long hair and wound it up in bobby pins so that it would survive the trek, and we drove to a little parking lot just off the freeway in the Hawaiian mountains. Ducking under a chain-link fence, we followed a path that wound over streams and huge boulders and sometimes stopped entirely with a dead end. After about thirty minutes, we rounded a bend to see a waterfall spilling from tall cliffs into a small pool below. Karla slipped into a silk dress with a bodice carefully threaded with small beads and

posed near the falls, her head tilted back with a gorgeous smile on her face. This was a glimpse of true beauty—an island girl who loved being herself.

My Story

One day I visited the Tower of London and caught an inspiring glimpse of how each woman is called to be herself in Christ.

I followed an ancient cobblestone path to a fantastic sight: the crown jewels of England. As I entered the treasury, the light dimmed and chatter hushed inside stone walls that guarded the wealth inside. A large movie screen dominated the first room, playing the coronation of Queen Elizabeth in 1953. My heart skipped a beat, captivated by the vintage movie.

Thousands of spectators flooded the streets to see the young woman who was about to step into her destiny. As the queen descended from her elaborate carriage, the band played, banners heralded her coming, and attendants gracefully bore the train of her mantle on her way to the throne. The queen took her position willingly, recognizing that she had not earned this right to rule by her own merit but that she had been born to inherit a crown. For her, accepting her position was not vanity or snobbery. This was who she was born to be, and refusing the honor would be ungrateful and arrogant. To be herself was to embrace her position and destiny.

Suddenly, I realized the film spoke of who we are in Christ. We are His beloved, a royal bride destined to rule and reign with Him, not because of any effort on our own but because He won this position for us. When we accept Christ's offer of eternal life, we become part of His kingdom, and we are seated with Christ in heavenly places. Christ longs for us to see ourselves the way He does and to step fully into our identity in Him. It is time to be ourselves—who the King says we are.

God's Story (Song of Sol. 1:5–10; 7:1; 1 Kings 1:3)

There are several scholarly perspectives regarding the Song of Solomon. The following narrative is woven around the view that Solomon fell in love with a young shepherdess from northern Israel who captured his heart like no other woman could.

⁓

"I am dark, but lovely," said the young maiden to herself with a slight flush. She looked at her skin, rough and tanned by the sun, not lily white like that of the finer ladies of her tribe. She had been working in the vineyard on the family farm ever since her brothers had made her prune the vines, and her hands were pricked, chapped, and slightly stained from the tart juice of grapes. Life in this Israelite farming community was simple, and the gently rolling hills and open pastureland were all that she had ever known. Into this world a man had come to win her heart and craft one of the greatest love stories of all time.

The young maiden from Shunem, called "Shulamite," smiled softly as she remembered the day she had met the king. He had entered their small town on official royal business, checking on the royal vineyard that stood adjacent to her father's. That morning she had been tending the vines when a friendly voice called from the other side of the low stone wall that bordered their field. "Well, hello there! I didn't realize I had company."

Shulamite looked up in surprise, embarrassed to be caught by a stranger in the field but curiously wondering who would boldly address a girl like herself. Solomon looked startled as he caught sight of her face, captivated by this young woman's obvious beauty.

"You are a beautiful sight this fine morning!" he quipped, throwing her a handsome smile.

"Not really," Shulamite responded with an awkward frown. "My brothers made me work in the vineyard, so I've really not taken care of myself." She untied the sleeves on her tunic, shaking them loose to hide her bronzed arms from the stranger. "I'm rather a mess."

"Not at all," the stranger replied, swinging over the fence that separated them. "I would say instead—" he paused, cocking his head to regard her with a small smile, "that you are dark . . . but lovely." His last words rang with soft admiration.

Shulamite looked at him, astonished. No man had ever spoken to her this way before. Her brothers were constantly arguing and rudely pushing her around, calling her by the pet name Abishag, meaning "our father's error," while her real name meant "peaceful." Now this handsome stranger was complimenting her, and she was at a loss for words. A noise in the vineyard interrupted their brief gaze, and the man looked behind him.

"I'd like to see you again," he said with a grin. "Will you be here tomorrow?"

Shulamite did a quick calculation. This man seemed safe, and certainly there wasn't any harm in seeing him out in the open.

"I'm keeping the sheep tomorrow," she offered. "Follow the footsteps of the flock from this field, and I'll be by the shepherds' tents."

"Until tomorrow, then," the stranger countered and disappeared among his own vines.

This was a first meeting of many, since the king's visit to the town seemed to be prolonged by more business. Shulamite remembered when she discovered that her new friend was actually the king and how her embarrassment deepened as she felt even uglier than before, comparing herself to the palace women. One day as they met in the forest behind her father's vineyard, she asked him, "Why do you want me in your life? The women of Jerusalem are much more beautiful than I."

The king smiled, pondering his muse as if to paint her in his mind. "I'm not comparing you to the city women," he replied, thinking how not one of the daughters of Jerusalem could compare to this simple, lovely shepherdess. "I would compare you to . . ." he deliberated as Shulamite waited with raised eyebrows, "a mare among Pharaoh's chariot horses," he finished.

"A horse? You'd not compare me to the palace women but to a horse?" She laughed, and King Solomon laughed with her.

"Those horses are the most noble beings you ever saw," he said, "decked with chains of gold and rows of jewels, proud and wild and free. In Pharaoh's army, all the horses are stallions, except the white mares that draw the king's chariot. If I were to compare you to anything, it would be to them." His eyes twinkled. "You can imagine how anxious the stallions are to follow Pharaoh's chariot into battle!"

Slowly, Shulamite began to notice that the king's way of seeing her was different from how she saw herself. She saw herself as dark; he said she was lovely. She compared herself to the palace women, but he compared her to the finest Arabian mares decorated with ropes of jewels. Her brothers called her "our father's error," but he called her "a prince's daughter." As she fell in love with this man, she began to see herself through his eyes. No longer was she the neglected little sister working in the vineyard. Instead, she was a woman pursued by the king! Just being herself was enough for him.

Solomon and Shulamite married and continued their life together, immortalized in the king's great love poem, the Song of Solomon. Never had the country girl dared to dream of living in the palace, but the king's love took her into an adventure beyond her wildest imagination.

◯◯◯

This tale of the shepherd girl and the king can be compared to the greatest love story ever: that of Christ's love for His bride, the church. As we unpack this beautiful account, we see some powerful reflections about true beauty.

Just like Shulamite, we sometimes struggle to see ourselves in the right perspective. Even on our best day, we don't come close to defining ourselves with the amazing wonder and creativity that God does. If we could catch one glimpse of how amazing we are in His eyes, we would never struggle with self-confidence again. Jesus longs to be the mirror we look into every day, to speak over us from His Word, and to remind us of the beauty that will never fade. We can start to see ourselves the way He does and be free to be ourselves.

We cannot earn Christ's love any more than a country girl had the power to earn the affection of a king. Rather, the King of Kings has simply fallen in love with us and madly pursues our hearts. He longs to speak beauty into our lives, and we simply get to be ourselves and enjoy Him, allowing His words to penetrate deeply into our hearts. As we embrace our identity in Christ, we realize this is who we are called to be. We are royalty in every way because Christ is our bridegroom King.

True Beauty Tip

Being ourselves is one of the secrets to true beauty, and the more we discover who Christ says we are, the more we can step into our destiny.

Questions for Reflection

1. Are you comfortable being yourself, or do you compare yourself to others?

2. Do you believe that God says you are beautiful? Is the idea difficult to receive?

3. Do you invite God into the messy places of your life, or do you try to earn His love before letting Him in?

4. Challenge yourself to find three friends and ask them, "What are some positive, unique traits you appreciate about me?" Then give them several words that describe your perspective of them too.

five

Beautiful Worth

You are the only you God made. . . . God made you and broke the mold.

—*Max Lucado*

Turning up the volume on the stereo, I listened to the heartfelt vocals of a young woman soar through my car. Katherine Chapman had just released her first single on a compilation album by worship artists in San Diego, California, and I was drawn to her song. As if writing a personal journal entry, she declared simply:

> I will follow
> I will pursue
> I will seek You
> Above any other
> Above any other god
> Above any other love
> Above any other name
> Jesus

I curiously wondered about the girl behind the song and how her journey had resulted in such a sweet display of love for her Savior. So I called Katherine (or Kat, as her friends call her) and asked to hear her story. Little did I know that behind these lyrics was a road of self-discovery and personal triumph that would rival any Hollywood movie plot. Our conversation uncovered many powerful keys of self-worth and carries invaluable hope for today's women.

As we filmed on a back porch in Southern California, I could immediately tell that Kat wanted nothing less than sincere authenticity in every part of her life—including our interview. She told her story with the same transparency with which she lived, daring to touch every emotion in its purest form and treasuring the sacredness of each one. She wanted me to meet her joy and pain and to feel at peace with both, because she was. With a playful sparkle in her eye, this beautiful woman shared her story of coming to understand the deep worth of her heart.

Kat's Story

Kat was a tomboy, a free-spirited soul who lived most of her childhood as a barefoot blonde in suburban San Diego. Her parents worked hard to make Christ the center of their home, where grace and forgiveness thrived, and they homeschooled Kat and her siblings all through their school-age years. Life wasn't a perfect utopia, since her father was ill for long periods of time and her mother worked up to four jobs at once to pay the bills. Yet even during the hard times, Kat and her siblings would often pile into the station wagon and drive across town with their mom to help someone in need. Kat's world was filled with an awareness of God, yet something inside her was unsure of how to succeed

at living for Him. A quiet child, she often withdrew into her own thoughts and locked her dreams inside her heart.

One day, squeezed between her siblings as they rode through town in the station wagon, Kat caught sight of a cardboard silhouetted ballerina in the window of a dance studio. With perfect poise, the dancer's graceful body delicately balanced in midair, a perfect emblem of womanhood to the young, dreamy child. Wide-eyed, the girl peeked out the window and dared to voice her dream to her family. "When I grow up, I want to be a ballerina," she declared.

One of her siblings scoffed, "You can't do that because ballerinas are pretty," inferring that she was disqualified from both her dream and the hope of beauty.

His words pierced Kat's soul like a jagged knife, and her shoulders slumped with dread. *I guess my dreams have no future because I'm not pretty*, she thought, a cold gray feeling settling over her thoughts, putting to death the wistful longing to be beautiful, known, and enjoyed. Determined to withhold her dreams and ambitions from further criticism, she sank into an introverted world where the voices of others carried more weight than her own. Kat became the wallflower who decided not to try hard at anything . . . especially at being beautiful.

So Kat became a tomboy, since boys accepted her companionship without comparison. It was easier to climb trees and be a chum than haggle with other girls for some undefined, unattainable place of being worthy of attention. Deep inside she wished she could be one of the pretty girls the boys adored, but she watched their romantic infatuations quickly fade and decided it wasn't worth the effort. She had always been told, "Don't be with a guy who just wants a pretty face, because he'll just leave when that outer beauty starts to fade." *Well*, she thought, *then I guess there's no reason to be attractive*. She decided it was easier to play it safe and avoid disappointment altogether.

Beauty still called to Kat, so she found ways to embrace it in her own way. As a teenager, she started to experiment with color, using markers to color her long blonde hair with rainbow stripes. Buying food coloring in bulk, she added the dye to hair gel and created hairstyles that were artistic and pretty. She loved to watch her hair gracefully swirl in the water with the dye; it was her personal idea of beauty that no one could compete with. One day her mom walked into the bathroom during a hairstyling moment and said, "Do you know why I let you do this? Not because coloring your hair makes you beautiful . . . but because you already are."

Kat appreciated the compliment, and she knew that her mom meant well, but she also had a nagging suspicion that her mom was only trying to make her feel good. Surfacing in her memory was a prank she and her brother had played on their mom as children, and the reminder filled her with doubt. One day she and her brother had had a conversation. "Do you ever notice that mom says everything looks great? Let's draw the ugliest picture we can make and see what she says."

With devilish glee, the siblings grabbed their markers and scribbled with haste, using browns and dark greens and pounding the felt tips onto the page. After concocting the most awful creation they could think of, they handed it to their optimistic mother.

"Mom, Mom! Look at what we made!"

Turning to observe the children's artwork, their mother automatically responded, "Wow, that's really pretty!"

Kat and her brother simultaneously burst into laughter and said, "No, it's not! It's ugly!"

Years later, standing in the bathroom with rainbow-colored hair, Katherine pondered, *Mom says I'm beautiful, but I guess she has to say that because she's my mom. Maybe she's just being nice; it's probably not really true.* Doubting her value was easier than believing she was beautiful.

In her quest for uniqueness, Kat turned to music. She loved singing with the worship team at church but often felt she was given the leftovers while the best parts went to those

> *Beauty is in the eye of the beholder, and it may be necessary from time to time to give a stupid or misinformed beholder a black eye.*
>
> —Miss Piggy

more important than she was. She wished she could be irreplaceable, but instead she felt as if her best efforts were never enough to please those around her, so eventually she simply stopped trying. A dark pattern of thoughts started winding its way into her mind. *You're not worthy. You don't really have anything valuable to contribute, so how dare you think you have something beautiful to offer God?*

One day Kat visited a church that had two worship leaders: a bald gentleman and a kind, authentic young guy named Rob. Every time the young man led worship, Kat's facade would crumble, and she would begin to weep as God touched her heart.

"Mom," she asked one day in church as the tears streamed down her face, "why do I cry each time that man plays a song?"

"I think you're sensing the Spirit of God," her mom responded. "That man has an anointing for worship. It's a gift from God to carry a song to the Lord." Little did Kat know that at the age of twenty-two she would marry Rob and they would devote their lives to ministry together.

For seven years of their marriage, the young couple plunged themselves into a new life of romance and building their dreams, but Kat still found nagging insecurities clinging to her mind. When she felt hurt, she shut down her emotions and smiled anyway. If she dreamed, she quickly downplayed her hopes, believing that she'd be disappointed. Even when tragedy struck, Kat undermined her grief, reminding herself that other people had

> *You can be gorgeous at thirty, charming at forty, and irresistible for the rest of your life.*
>
> —Coco Chanel

things worse than she did. Gritting her teeth in determination, Kat stubbornly refused to succumb to her emotions even when they were screaming to be heard. Rather than grapple with the lies, she decided to stop singing and pursuing beauty and simply shut down her heart, stoically wading through the motions of life.

The couple had two babies, and then Kat began to miscarry. This was a new, indescribable depth of pain, and she suddenly felt like a failure at the one thing she desperately wanted to achieve: being a good mom. She had seven miscarriages, four of them in one year, and each time she lost a baby, another blow hit her aching heart. Grief swept over her like a tsunami as she thought, *I can't even care for my babies!*

One day, during her eighth pregnancy, Kat's resolve was pushed to the breaking point. Life was hard, financial struggles were constant, the family business wasn't going well, and keeping food on the table was difficult. Frustration welled up as Kat wrestled with feelings of inadequacy. No matter how hard she tried to follow advice or to give everything she had, it was never enough. *There must be something wrong with me,* she reasoned with shame. *I feel like I can't even please God. Why won't He bless me?*

On top of this, Kat's instincts told her that something was wrong with the baby. With no insurance and her husband away from the house, she drove to the hospital and checked herself in. Doctors confirmed the truth: the baby had no heartbeat. Again the old pain rose up in Kat—an indescribable sense of grief and shame. She went home and delivered the baby naturally—all alone. That night she held the tiny body of her miscarried child in her hands and decided to honor its short life by giving it an honorable burial.

Under the cover of darkness, she slipped into the yard and dug a small grave. She wrapped the tiny body in a cloth as tears flooded her face and dripped onto the ground.

"I'm so sorry we had to meet this way," she whispered to the tiny child, "but you are loved and wanted."

Her emotions overflowed, and Kat couldn't hold them back any longer. Gritty dirt clinging to her fingers, the numb cold of the evening, the ache of her childless womb—it was more than she could bear. She felt so human and out of control, and yet little wispy thoughts still played in her mind. *Someone in the world has life much worse than you,* they ranted. *A woman in a third-world country may not even have the time to stop and grieve her child . . . she would have to bury her pain and keep working to put food on the table. So just be strong and deal with it.*

The next day life went on as usual, but Kat's emotions were still spiraling into depression. As she drove to the store, the car's dashboard lights came on; she realized the engine was in trouble, and there was no money for a mechanic.

"God, just let another car hit me," she prayed in despair. "I don't have any money to fix this, so maybe you could send an accident so insurance could take care of it."

Nothing happened, and as she pulled into her driveway, her tears started to flow.

"Lord, You don't meet my needs through Your goodness, and You won't even use tragedy to meet my needs," she sobbed. Feeling completely broken and abandoned, Kat slipped into the house and sat down with Rob for an honest talk.

"I don't want to be God's weak, needy little girl who can't make things work," she shared in frustration. "Why does everything bad happen at once? Why can't a thousand dollars just appear in my bank account to help us out?"

Rob turned to her and said, "Maybe that's been it all along: God wants you to be His little girl. He just wants us to let Him love us— not because we have something to offer but just because we're His."

Suddenly, Kat realized that she had been trying to earn worth in God's sight by being strong and having everything together, but instead of feeling worthy, the shame was unbearable when she couldn't hold things together. This time she didn't have any strength to make life pretty, but if she could let go of her struggle just a little, maybe she could rest in God's arms and let Him love her.

That night she posted on social media, "I lost the baby. Please don't tell me you're sorry, because that just haunts me with memories. Instead, please just let me know that you love me."

To her shock, encouragement and affirmation came flooding from friends near and far as many voiced their love and support. She realized she didn't have to downplay the hurt, because no one was expecting her to be strong, and she could be honest with her heart. Her pain was valid, and the hurt was real, but this time she could receive comfort. To her shock, one woman even added a thousand dollars to Kat's bank account!

From that day forward, Kat began to see God's goodness in her life. When she was raw and open with her feelings—both the good and the bad—she could receive God's comfort in the pain and joy in the beauty. Slowly, she started to realize that she had painted God into the shape of something He was not. The disasters had not been caused by Him; rather, He had been reaching through each difficulty and waiting for her to stop trying to earn His affection. Her worth was not found in whether she could prove herself to God or in competing with others for the best portion. She could rest in the fact that God had already proven His love for her on the cross, and He was present in every circumstance.

One day in the shower, Kat began to pinpoint the battlefield in her mind. Itemizing the lies that tormented her, she began to call them out.

Fear: I'm afraid of singing in front of a microphone, terrified that I won't be good enough.

Doubt: What if God doesn't meet my needs?

Hopelessness: Am I valuable enough to merit God's love?

Comparison: What if someone "does life" better than I do?

Abandonment: Do I attract God's attention, or do I have to fight for it?

As the water poured down her face, Kat decided to worship God, daring to sing in the face of every lie that dared to raise its ugly head. "I will bow my knee only to You, God," she vowed.

"These other 'gods,' the lies that want my attention, are not going to win! I want You above any other affection, delight, or loyalty, above any other spotlight or position—even a ministry position. I'm going to start singing from my heart as a little child, and I don't care what anyone thinks."

There in the shower, she began to sing these words:

> I will follow
> I will pursue
> I will seek You
> Above any other
> Above any other god
> Above any other love
> Above any other name
> Jesus

Later that day, she sat down with Rob, and together they put guitar chords to the song she had written in the shower. Rob sang the tune when leading worship at church, and people began to embrace the chorus and sing along. No one knew Kat was the author, and she refused to tell. Mostly, she thought people in church were just singing out of obligation, but soon she had to admit that they were truly worshiping and that God was using her song. Birthed by pain and difficulty, the chorus resonated in a greater way than she could have imagined. Eventually, Kat slipped out of obscurity and braved the stage, confessing that she was the author and choosing to sing it herself. Her song "Above Any Other" was recorded by a citywide worship movement and is now sung in various countries around the world.

Today Kat is a mother of five healthy children and serves at the church where her husband is on staff as worship pastor. She admits that life isn't always easy, but now she sees things with fresh eyes.

"As a girl, I thought beauty was being in control, feeling strong, and having no sign of weakness," she shared. "Now the most attractive thing to me is peace, joy, being at rest, and being able to see the best in things. I also realize that what you pay a high price for has greater equity. I choose not to give up even in the hard times. I want the fire to create something beautiful in me . . . something of great value."

Kat started singing again, but this time she was not trying to be heard, competing for attention, or afraid of blending in. Now she sings because her heart is full and overflowing with gratitude to her Savior. No one can talk her out of her value, because it doesn't come from any other human being. True worth and value come from knowing that you are loved and accepted by the God of the universe and choosing to bow the knee to Him alone.

Photo Shoot

For Kat's before photos, we drove to the little ballet studio that still has cardboard silhouettes of dancers in the window. We photographed in the busy street below, and on her cardboard scraps she penned in curvy calligraphy the words INVISIBLE, MEDIOCRE, and NUMB. Then we tore up those words and left them in the trash.

Her after photos were much more fun. I wanted to shoot a music video to Kat's song "Above Any Other," so she wore a flowing dress of deep blue and we met at a California beach with a ballet dancer. Sporting a tutu of elegant pink, she danced to Kat's song while waves crashed on cliffs behind us, and we celebrated the beauty that comes from embracing our value in Christ.

My Story

A knock on the front door interrupted the afternoon with a glad surprise. It was Pete, our mailman, who had paused on his route for a quick moment of encouragement. Once in a while, he would just pop in, deliver the mail by hand, and let us know he was praying for us. At this time in my life, I had just graduated from high school without much clarity for the next season, so he spent a couple minutes chatting with me about the future.

"I'd really like to do some kind of ministry work," I divulged, "but I know I'm just a girl."

Somehow I had picked up the notion that God liked to send men to the mission field more than women and that half of the human race was designated to clean houses and do laundry as their primary purpose.

"I don't mind being God's second choice," I said nobly, "but I would really like to do something for Him."

Pete's eyes grew wide with fatherly concern, and his gray beard softened as he smiled. "Rebecca," he said, "you're not God's second choice for anything. He has a very special calling for *you*."

I was shocked. *Really? God values* me *just as I am? I'm not second best?* Suddenly, I gained courage to dream big, fly high, and love without limits. It was a moment of awakening, a dare to believe the impossible and find it true, all because someone had released God's value over my life. The kindness of a mailman fueled the passion to dream inside a fearful teenage girl. Discovering your true worth always gives wings to the soul.

God's Story (Luke 15:1–10)

The Jewish rabbi watched the shuffle of feet and clouds of dust as people tried to find a place close enough to hear His words. For days, crowds had been following Him through Galilee in hopes of hearing one of His thought-provoking messages that pierced their souls. Even the outcasts of society were curiously seeking Him out. Tax collectors and women whose questionable character was openly known were pressing through the masses, hoping to listen to this man.

Jesus knew that not everyone in the crowd was excited by the presence of these outcasts. Annoyed, the religious leaders squinted with disdain and murmured under their breath, "Look at this rabble! Rabbi, You'd better watch Your company!"

Jesus instantly perceived their concerns. Compassion welled up as He watched the seekers mingle around Him, desperate for authentic leadership. Looking up into the hills, He gestured to a shepherd leading his flock along the top of a ravine. "Suppose one of you had a hundred sheep," He began, knowing that many in the crowd were shepherds, "and one was lost. Wouldn't you leave the ninety-nine in the wilderness and search high and low until you found it?"

He held their attention as they wondered what He meant. *Of course we would attempt to rescue our livestock!* they thought.

Jesus smiled at a woman in the hushed crowd, remembering His own mother's frantic search for lost things when He was a boy, and told another story. "Imagine a woman who has ten coins and loses one. Don't you think she'll spend all night looking in every nook and cranny until she finds it? Even if she has to light a lamp and stay up late, she won't rest until it's found. When she finds it, she will call her friends to tell them the good news, saying, 'Celebrate with me! The lost coin has been found!'"

Jesus turned to face the crowd, who listened with rapt attention. He threw back His head and laughed, declaring with joy, "This is how God feels about you! There is so much joy in heaven when one lost child comes home."

The people caught their breath in wonder. Were they really valued by God? Did He really long for their company? The religious leaders squinted and frowned. The sinners blinked back tears. Jesus just smiled, knowing that the Father was about to paint a bigger picture of love than anyone had yet dreamed of. God loved the world so much that He sent His Son to find the lost sheep and missing coins—even though the cost was great. Ah yes, each of these listeners—from ragamuffins to scholars—was of deep worth to the Father.

∽⁊∾

God passionately searches for us and won't rest until we are home. He compares His search to that of a desperate woman who can't sleep because she has lost a precious treasure. That is how persistently He pursues His children. If we could understand how deeply valued we are by Him, how quickly we would respond to His love. The greatest of all stories is that Christ Jesus left heaven in pursuit of us and returned with the warrior scars of victory, reuniting us with God. When we embrace the tremendous sacrifice of love poured out on our behalf, we truly understand how valuable we are. The King of heaven gave His life in our place, taking our sin, shame, and guilt upon Himself so that we could freely receive His love.

True Beauty Tip

Our value doesn't depend on whether this world notices us, or even if we feel good about ourselves. True value rests on the fact that our Creator is madly in love with His creation and longs to be intimately connected with us. Our value and worth are unconditional. However, we will experience the fullness of the Creator's love only when we are in relationship with the God who made us. Like any relationship, this relationship doesn't happen on its own. We have to invite Him into our lives. When we do, our true worth unfolds in a beautiful way.

Questions for Reflection

1. What are some moments when you have felt "less than"?
2. What does it mean to enjoy beauty because you are already beautiful rather than trying to attain it?
3. Jesus loved you enough to die for you. What does this tell you about your worth to Him?
4. God searches the house like a woman who lost her coin. What does this say about how much He values you?

six

Beautiful Trust

I keep telling myself that I'm a human being, an imperfect human being who's not made to look like a doll, and that who I am as a person is more important than whether at that moment I have a nice figure.

—*Emma Watson*

The vivid, panoramic view was so breathtaking that I caught my breath with sheer delight. Looking like a storybook cover, bleating lambs and doting ewes dotted the lush English countryside, and huge jackrabbits nibbled and manicured the grass into a cropped carpet. To my right, the land abruptly dropped, bordered by a shoreline of white cliffs, where waves crashed into rocky shores below. I felt as if I were on an epic movie set and wondered if Jane Austen was about to gracefully step out from the past and enter the scene. Instead, another young author walked with me, journal in hand. Amy, a thoughtful and charming young woman, was the perfect guide, since this was her childhood home. Set

91

against this romantic backdrop, her story calls all of us to a place of deeper trust in our Creator.

I had a difficult time imagining that anything harmful could ever happen in this romantic, storybook field, but Amy confided that Beachy Head, one of the chalky white cliffs that overlooked the sea, was dubbed "Suicide Cliff." An estimated twenty people a year jump the 530 feet to their deaths in the icy water below, making this the site of the third largest number of suicides in the world. A chaplaincy team conducts daily patrols to watch for potential jumpers, and the Coast Guard regularly retrieves bodies from the shoreline below. I couldn't fathom that Amy, a vibrant brunette with a vivacious passion for life, had ever contemplated this path, so I listened closely as she honestly shared her story. It offers us a peek into her heart and helps us discover the keys to beautiful trust.

Amy's Story

The moment ten-year-old Amy discovered she was assigned to Mr. Jones's class for her last year of primary school, her heart sank. Amy had always been a good student, but rumors about Mr. Jones sent waves of dread pounding through her mind. Demanding absolute perfection from the students, the teacher enjoyed intimidating and shaming the children in front of the entire class, and the students shared whispered horror stories of his punishment tactics. Amy decided that she would do everything in her power to avoid criticism, so she entered his class with the determination to win his favor. To her dismay, the stories of this bullying teacher turned out to be true.

"You're useless! You should be ashamed of yourself," he shouted as he leaned over a child with a scowl. "Don't you dare tell your

parents what I'm saying, because I will find you and come after you."

Terrified, Amy silently vowed that she would always please him. If perfection was required, she would make sure she achieved it no matter the cost—but the bullying continued. She spent hours on her homework assignments only to be given a zero even when her answers were correct. The mean-spirited teacher refused to mark her present for class, so the school cafeteria did not prepare a hot lunch for her. Instead of complaining, she brought a sack lunch to school to avoid any conflict.

One day Amy's father slipped into the classroom and saw the way Mr. Jones towered over the small children and shouted belittling comments at them. He was horrified and wanted to talk to the teacher, but Amy begged him not to. She knew what he did to children whose parents complained, and she couldn't stand the thought of what he might do to her. Despite her silence, eventually enough students exposed the truth and the teacher was expelled, but not before he left an imprint on one student: Amy was terrified of humiliation.

Amy adored her parents, strong Christians who desired to build a safe home for their children. But after her experience with Mr. Jones, her simple longing to please others turned into an insatiable need to perform. Terrified that her best would never be good enough, Amy carried these harmful words in her heart: "I will always let everyone down" and "It would be better if I could just disappear." *If I can find a way to please everyone perfectly*, she mused, *I'll never have to endure humiliation again.* In hopes of protecting her tender heart, Amy made strict promises to herself:

I am never going to fail again.

I must never accept anything below perfection in my life.

Amy shared how these inner precepts dictated her life. "These words followed me into my teenage life and began to cause deeper problems. My teacher's voice daily replayed in my head, and his words became self-fulfilling prophecies. I began to demand of myself things that were impossible to achieve. I vowed never to allow anyone to make me feel the way he had, and this kick-started a need to control absolutely everything in my life."

Even with the abusive teacher gone, life continued to throw Amy curveballs she didn't know how to handle. When she was twelve, her parents were shocked to discover they were expecting a baby. Amy shifted into high gear, desperately wanting everyone to be happy, so she took it upon herself to do as much as possible to help around the house. After the birth of her brother, her mom was diagnosed with postpartum depression, so Amy sent her mom to bed every afternoon, did the housework, and watched her brother. She became obsessed with germs, preparing food plans, and keeping everything clean. Fear drove her, and soon her desire to achieve turned into an obsession to control.

When the baby was only six months old, an unexpected blow hit the family: Amy's grandmother developed lung cancer and died within two weeks. Amy confided, "It had happened so quickly, everyone was so sad, and I hated it. I felt very out of control with everything that was happening in my life. First my teacher, then a new baby brother, and now my only grandparent had died. I became very afraid that someone else in my family would die, and this fueled my obsession of making sure everyone was resting and eating well while I took care of them."

Life was spinning out of control, and Amy grappled for something solid to hold on to. As a young teenager, she became a prime target for anorexia, the eating disorder that causes its victims to starve their bodies, often due to an obsessive desire to manage something tangible when life seems out of control. Many girls with anorexia weigh themselves frequently, exercise excessively, and eat only small amounts of food.

Amy's obsession with being thin started innocently. Amy often tagged along to her mom's postnatal group and enjoyed fussing over the babies, but surrounded by new moms, she overheard them talking about the latest diets and how to lose their post-baby weight. It seemed that everyone's goal was to become thin and happy, and Amy began to wonder if this could be true for her too. In the supermarket, she became fascinated by the skeletal models who sparkled with appealing smiles on magazine covers. Manically flipping through the pages, she found stories about diets and celebrity food plans. Comparing her teenage body to the magazine icons, she began to feel disgusted with herself and filled with guilt that she weighed more than they did. The guilt and shame of being less than the best was too much to take, and she decided that life would be better if she was thinner. *Perhaps*, she reasoned, *being thin will make me happy, just like these models seem to be.*

Before long, she was obsessed with food. In the grocery store, she insisted on reading nutritional labels to discover how many calories each item contained. Food started making her feel ugly, so more and more often, Amy simply didn't eat and exercised more. She was hooked on this new lifestyle, but somehow it didn't help her inner torment but rather fed it. Fighting with her family over food, she discovered she wasn't the perfect daughter anymore and felt she was letting everyone down. Now she couldn't even control whether they liked her. In an attempt to cope with even more misery, she looked for a way to endure the pain. She shared, "Cutting became another form of venting the disgust, hatred, guilt, and shame that I felt. Pretty soon I was keeping knives up in my room to deal with the pain. It became a temporary fix, a rush of adrenaline, and a brief distraction. All my life I'd wanted nothing more than to be the perfect daughter and to make my parents proud of me, but in my desire for perfection and control, I had become this unrecognizable monster who was causing all manner of hurt

> *Anorexia, you starve yourself. . . . You just deny yourself. It's about control.*
>
> —Tracey Gold

and pain every single day. Mostly, cutting was about punishing myself."

With increasing pain, Amy brutally chastised herself for the guilt she carried, much like the tormenting bullying she had received from her abusive teacher. She began to be a merciless taskmaster, demanding incessant perfection no one could live up to. Wanting to please everyone, yet feeling like a constant disappointment, she wondered if her family might be better off without her. She felt completely out of control—and it frightened her.

One day she hiked up to Beachy Head, the suicide point where so many had taken their lives. The grass was poetically green, the grazing sheep were surreal and peaceful, but the countryside did nothing to soothe the troubled girl. Wind whipped her face as she stepped to the edge of the bluff and looked out to sea, wondering if she should jump. Suddenly, she felt a presence, as if an unseen hand was pulling her back from the edge. Something shifted ever so slightly in her soul, challenging the brooding agony with a calm reminder that she was still loved. A gentle quietness filled her that had nothing to do with the soothing landscape, and she experienced a quiet resolution that her life was not yet finished. As she walked from the cliffs, she believed she had been handed a second chance at life.

Shortly after this, Amy heard of a Christian residential program for girls and decided to go to the center farther north in England. "It was the first day of the rest of my life, really," she confided.

Like skilled physicians removing old bandages from a wound, the counselors peeled off the layers of lies that masked Amy's true heart. Baring her soul, Amy realized that the battle for her life was ongoing and her peace was at stake. Was she going to

surrender to God and believe that He was willing and able to help, or was she going to keep trying to fix her life by manipulating everything?

One day a staff member led her to a window and pulled back the curtain to unveil the English moors. Rolling hills spread as far as she could see, and sunshine spilled through ivory clouds that hovered close to the ground. Amy soaked in the beauty of the landscape.

"If God made all this," her counselor said tenderly, gesturing to the outdoor beauty, "can't He take care of your problems?" She lifted Amy's hand, turning it so her palm faced the sky. "Your troubles are just a speck in His hand, easily cared for by the Creator of the universe. He will hold them if you trust Him."

Suddenly, Amy realized that her entire journey had brought her to this point. Either she could keep controlling things and head down a dangerous road of hurting herself and others, or she could trust God to carry the load for her. She didn't have to please everyone or fix everything; that was God's job. He was inviting her to let go of the weight of her problems and put them in His care, believing that He saw, understood, and would do His part to take care of things that were bigger than she was. Like a little child, Amy reached for her Father's hand and decided to trust Him.

Probing deeper, she began to see how the personal decrees she had chosen as a young child had embedded themselves into her soul. Instead of trusting her Father, she had become bent on proving her worth to those around her and to herself. Writing down each lie, she began to counter them with truth.

Remember always that you not only have the right to be an individual, you have an obligation to be one.

—Eleanor Roosevelt

Lie: I am never going to fail again.

Truth: I will make mistakes, but I am still loved. When needed, I will forgive myself.

Lie: I must never accept anything below perfection in my life.

Truth: I will do my best and aim high, but my identity is not based on success.

Lie: I will always let everyone down.

Truth: I am not responsible for everyone, so I will make healthy boundaries and expectations that I can reasonably achieve.

Lie: It would be better if I could just disappear.

Truth: I am valuable and wonderfully made by God, and He has a plan for my life.

Brick by brick, Amy began to tear down the old thoughts and rebuild her mind-set based on the truth of God's Word. Even though freedom was a battle, her weapons were sharp and she knew she could win. For the first time, excitement welled up, joy carried over into her smile again, and her heart regained its strength. She didn't have to control everything in order to feel safe—she could simply do her part and trust God with the rest.

After completing the program, Amy returned to her family's home on the coast. She took long walks by the cliffs, but now she enjoyed the beauty of the serene pastureland without being lulled into danger. Each spring new lambs bleated in the fields, and fresh flowers burst into bloom around the old stone hedges, reminding her that life could begin again. As she hiked the familiar hills, Amy smiled with a new peace in her eyes, soaking in the sunshine of a new day and trusting God to care for all He had made—even her.

Today Amy is free from eating disorders and depression and enjoys a healthy life as a childcare worker. Ten years after her life-threatening addiction, she shared, "There have been good days and bad days, but slowly the good days began to outweigh the bad ones. I've learned to talk about my struggles and not keep them bottled up inside me until they reach the point of explosion. Accountability is key to recovery, and I am very blessed to have my mum, who I can talk to about anything. Occasionally,

I have moments of struggle, but these are extremely rare now, and when they do arise, I have healthy ways of dealing with them. I'm excited about the future and look forward to God's plan for my life!"

Photo Shoot

We started Amy's shoot on the busy streets of West London, where the blur of heavy traffic and littered streets made a harsh backdrop for her before photos. I snapped shots as she held cardboard signs that read CONTROLLED, FEARFUL, and ALONE.

For her makeover, we jumped on the train and headed to the English coast, where I stepped into Amy's paradise: the beautiful pastureland and white cliffs of East Sussex. After filming at the top of the bluffs, Amy dressed in a gorgeous blue dress and we drove to the beach, where waves pounded the rocks. Somewhere on this shoreline, the victims of many suicides have been found, but this day told a different story, because a young woman stood dressed in beauty, triumphantly holding a new sign that read FREEDOM.

My Story

Letting go of control and trusting God can be downright hard sometimes, but the rewards are beautiful as we watch Him show up as only He can. I discovered this at the age of twenty-three when I was still living at home and longing to do something beautiful with my life. A nagging thought kept popping up in my mind: *What if I rent a studio apartment and spend a year seeking Jesus and creating various art forms that glorify Him?* I had already been speaking in churches for about a year, and I had the opportunity to intern at a church in the area, so I decided to go for it—at least until I came up with a better idea.

Soon I stumbled upon a garage apartment for rent. The moment I walked in, I wanted to cry. It was perfect! This was my studio—a place I could live, create, and pray with abandon. So I signed the lease for a year, bought some thrift store furniture, and pursued my ministry calling with the stubborn belief that somehow God would make a way for me to pay my bills.

The first month I didn't make enough income to pay my rent and I had to pull it from my savings account. Maybe this sounds silly, but I was absolutely crushed. *Perhaps I'm not called to ministry life after all,* I wondered. *What if God isn't going to take care of me?*

Doubts plagued my mind, and I shed some tears, trying to figure out how to remedy the situation. To be honest, I was terrified that my step of faith might turn out to be a complete failure.

One day I heard the quiet voice of Jesus speak to my thoughts, "Rebecca, who is on the throne of your heart? Is it Me or your emotions?"

Shocked, I realized that my panicked feelings were absorbing my time, and I wasn't trusting God. Emotions are important, but at that moment, mine were running rampant and dominating my life with fear. I realized that I could either continue to let them rule or make them trade places with the King of Kings and trust that He was going to make a way. So I simply asked Him to forgive me for allowing my emotions to rule and to take the throne of my heart. I knew that whatever happened, He would show me what to do next.

Over the next thirty days, I didn't make a lot of money, but nearly every day someone paid for a meal. I didn't tell anyone about my needs—things just happened naturally. Day after day, I received spontaneous invitations to eat meals in homes around a kitchen table or in restaurants, and I never had to pay a dime. My heavenly Father and I had a delightfully private joke as I trusted Him to provide food every day. As a result, my grocery bill was very low, and by the end of the month, I was able to pay my rent. After those thirty days, I started making more money, and the invitations abruptly stopped. This was an amazing time when God tenderly taught me how to make room for His love in my life by simply trusting Him. If I had spent time trying to control the situation, I would have missed His provision and the fun of watching Him show up.

If I am honest, I'll admit that sometimes I try to control situations and help things along instead of bringing God into the equation and simply doing my part. The lie is that it is up to us to make things work. God is ready to partner with us and accomplish more than we could ever do on our own. Trust is required, and we have to let go of the steering wheel to let Him drive. He is a much better driver than we are and knows what is best.

God's Story (Matt. 14:14–32)

Sinking low behind towering hills, the sun cast its last rays of rose-colored light over the day. Thousands of people filled the Galilean countryside, where soft, grassy knolls created a natural amphitheater where Jesus could teach. It seemed nearly everyone in the seaside village towns had abandoned their work to see this new teacher, and they had not been disappointed. Signs and wonders had shocked the crowds as many sick people were healed, and they had all received a free lunch when Jesus multiplied a couple fish and a few loaves of bread to feed thousands.

In awe, the people clamored for Jesus's attention, and His disciples were constantly busy caring for the crowd. Passing the bread to everyone, helping the sick form a line to get to Jesus, and making sure no one harmed the Master . . . it had been a long day, and they were exhausted. That evening Jesus called them and said, "Get into the fishing boat and go to the other side of the lake. I'll meet you there later."

Sweating and tired, the disciples clambered into the boat, pushed off with rugged oars, and launched into the sea. They basked in the calm of the evening as the boat glided through silent waters. Suddenly, the wind rose with a howl, and the men jumped to their feet, alarmed at the storm that had come out of nowhere. Waves pummeled the sides of the boat and crashed over the prow, until even the hardened sailors of the group feared for their lives.

Just before dawn, one of them cried out in terror, pointing to a strange sight even more terrifying than the storm: a figure was walking toward them on the waves!

"It's a ghost!" they shouted, clinging to the creaking boat that threatened to capsize. Cutting through the howling wind, a voice they knew well reached their ears.

"Be of good courage," Jesus called. "It's Me. Don't be afraid!"

Peter was the first of the disciples to recover his voice. "Lord, if it's really You," he dared the Master, "call me to come walk with You on the waves!"

Jesus, laughing as the wind and water whipped the terrified men, responded, "Come!"

To his own astonishment, Peter found himself stepping out of the boat, his feet securely resting on the top of the water. His jaw dropped with wonder, and he looked at the Lord with laughter as the storm raged around them. One step . . . then another. Peter was walking on water, just like Jesus! Suddenly, a crack of thunder sounded just above his head, and a tremendous wave hurled itself toward the boat, knocking everyone to their knees. Peter tore his eyes away from the laughing gaze of Christ and looked back to the wall of water that was quickly rolling his way.

I'm in the middle of the sea with nothing to hold on to, he thought, groping for a lifeline but finding nothing. The water began to spurt up between his toes. Then it rolled over his ankles. He was sinking! Peter reached back toward the boat, but it was too far away to be of any help. By this time the water had risen above his knees. Panicking, Peter started clawing the water in a desperate attempt to swim, but the waves were closing in with alarming speed and filling his mouth with water. "Lord," he cried with a gasp, "help me!"

Immediately, the warm hand of the Master closed around his arm, and Jesus pulled Peter to his feet.

"You have such little faith," He admonished Peter as they made their way to the boat. As soon as they stepped inside, the storm stopped raging and the wind died into a pleasant whisper, bowing at the feet of its King. With intense compassion and just a hint of sadness, the Lord looked into Peter's shocked eyes and asked, "Why did you doubt Me?"

Peter, the rough seaman, fought back tears as he observed the Master's disappointment. As the sky brightened with a hint of dawn, he pondered how trusting the Lord was even more important than trying to navigate the crashing waves. He realized that Christ had everything under control and all that was required of Peter was to get out of the boat and trust Him.

True Beauty Tip

Trusting God brings peace. It works more miracles for our complexion than any cosmetic by easing panic lines and removing creases of worry. Even in the midst of chaos beyond our control, Christ calmly stands in the middle of the waves, unmoved by the drama. "Come," He says. "Trust Me in the middle of this uncontrollable situation. Don't be afraid—just keep your eyes on Me." Trusting Him is the key not only to surviving the waves but also to walking with Him through any storm. Trust is a beautiful thing.

Questions for Reflection

1. In what area do you struggle the most with trusting God?

2. What are the "waves" or the fearful situations in your life that distract you?

3. Are you secure in the Father's love, or do you struggle to earn it by performing for Him?

4. Are there areas in your life where you are overly controlling and you need to trust God more? Explain them and bring them before God in prayer.

seven

Beautiful Exchange

You have to let go of who you were to allow yourself to become who you are.

—*Stacy London*

I will confess my weakness: I am addicted to makeover TV shows! I could watch them all day long, because seeing transformation dawn on a human being never gets old. The moment a woman nervously faces the mirror after a stylist works her magic and gasps in shock at her reflection is priceless. She may have labeled herself ordinary, plain, or even damaged goods, but the stylist obviously saw something of far more value in her. Suddenly, the wallflower is transformed into a princess who holds her head high, recognizes her value, and is ready to pursue her dreams.

Sometimes there is a twist: the Cinderella chosen for a makeover may be required by the fairy godmother to turn in her old wardrobe first, so piece by piece, they sort through the clothes that are too big as well as the too-small clothes she dreams of fitting into. The woman lets the stylist sweep through her wardrobe because she knows the stylist holds two powerful keys: the vision to see her potential and a gift card to purchase an amazing new wardrobe.

God is a great stylist. Like a father watching his young daughter attempt to dress herself, He must be amused when we try to fit into outfits never made with us in mind. Just like outdated clothes still claim a place in our closets, old attitudes, behaviors, and inner beliefs take up space in our minds, even though they are ugly and don't represent our identity as children of the King. We hold on to dreams we have outgrown, hand-me-down expectations from others, and even dirty laundry from past mistakes. Our heavenly Father whispers, "Daughter, do you know who you are? You are My child. I value you enough to give you royal robes of honor, dignity, and real love. Will you trade your old life for a new one? Will you trust Me long enough to let it all go?" The struggle is real, but the reward is priceless.

Nowhere did I see this idea of God's makeover illustrated more powerfully than in the story of a young fashion stylist in Mexico. Her journey of trading old for new reveals a profound picture of how God presents us with the great exchange. After I drove to Mexico, Lizbeth was waiting for me at the mission house in Ensenada, excitedly pushing long, dark hair from her beaming face. She welcomed me with a warm hug, and I followed her to an empty room in the stucco hotel turned mission, which sat only a block from a sandy, white beach. I wondered what had brought this young fashion stylist from the runways of Los Angeles to the shores of Mexico. What followed was the real-life story of how God crafts a makeover.

Lizbeth's Story

Lizbeth's father left home before she was born, and her mother was consumed with grief over his absence. Alcohol and smoking fed her depression until a strange conviction made her stop, but the substance abuse had taken a toll, and Lizbeth was born with a hole in her heart. The physical gap closed by itself, but an emotional hole soon began to grow in the young child as her absent father slipped in and out of her life. Although still married to her mother, he didn't live in the home and rarely spent time in his daughter's world. Dark thoughts began to wrap around Lizbeth's childhood mind as her life started spiraling downward.

Unwanted—This lie stuck in her mind like a burr caught on a fine silk dress. Someone told her that her father left home for good when he discovered that his new child was a girl. He had wanted a son, and Lizbeth had been a disappointment. *Do I have any value?* she wondered, not knowing how to cope with the answer.

Dirty—Unprotected and vulnerable, Lizbeth was molested as a little girl, and she felt it was all her fault. Her mother moved between homes in Mexico and Los Angeles, and Lizbeth was sexually abused in both countries by different perpetrators. After four years, the eight-year-old girl courageously stood up to her abusers and said no. The abuse stopped, but nobody knew about it. It was a chilling secret she locked away for years.

Not good enough—When she was ten years old, she and her cousin were playing with Barbie dolls one day when a car pulled into the driveway. Her cousin jumped up, saying, "I want to say hello to my uncle." Lizbeth peeked out the window, horrified to see her father and five other children getting out of the car. Although her parents were still married, her father had moved in with another woman and was raising another family. Immediately, Lizbeth wondered why she was not valuable enough for her father to want her. *If I had been good enough for him,* she told herself, *perhaps he would have been the father I long for. Obviously, I am not good enough.*

While holding these lies in her heart, the charm of the fashion industry began to tug at Lizbeth. She loved dressing up, and she dreamed of working behind the scenes as a stylist or a stage co-ordinator at a fashion runway. Outer beauty became her means of coping with inner chaos, and she also found value in bringing beauty to others. Her family members asked her to do their hair and makeup for special events, and soon this became a real way that she could reach out to others. Maybe she didn't feel beautiful or treasured, but she could make others feel lovely and bring joy to them in this way. Somehow this beauty enabled her to cope with the aching absence of her value.

Unbeknown to Lizbeth, a greater Love was wooing and pursuing her. Ultimately, this Love held the balm that would heal her heart—not just cover up the pain. One day Lizbeth went to youth camp and heard about Jesus Christ.

"If you come to Jesus," the preacher said, "He can erase all of your past. You can be clean and have a new life."

Lizbeth desperately wanted to feel pure, so she ran to the altar, committed her life to Christ, and was baptized. It was the start of a new journey, and now each time the lies whispered, "You're unworthy, dirty, and not good enough," another voice whispered, "That's not true." She knew that Jesus had washed those lies away. The divine makeover had begun, and Lizbeth began to let go of the old baggage and choose to believe that Jesus had made her pure and saw her differently.

After graduating from high school, Lizbeth began to work as a wardrobe stylist for a designer. Her love for beauty and people made her one of the top sales workers on the floor, and her confidence began to increase. Slowly, her faith also grew as she read the Bible in her room and prayed. Every Sunday she went to church, where the message pierced her heart and she wept with joy.

God has dreams for me, she realized with deep gratitude. *He has brought me through so much, and I am His daughter.* The heart makeover swung into full gear as she shed her old identity like moth-eaten rags and wrapped herself in a new perspective.

Loved—God deeply treasures and values me, not because I am perfect but because He created me and is truly proud of what He has made.

Chosen—A destiny is waiting for me, and I was created with a special purpose in mind.

Valued—I am no longer thrown aside like a worn-out rag doll. God treasures me every day of my life.

Like a dry, brittle sponge, Lizbeth soaked in the truth of God's grace, choosing to wear her Father's words in her heart and mind. One day she realized that God was asking her to extend this mercy to others too and that she needed to forgive her dad for his absence in her life. This realization brought her to a fork in the road: she could either hold on to the past like a basket of dirty laundry or allow the Father to give her a new start. Was she willing to forgive her father and let go of the hurt? Bitterness had been her constant companion, like an old, itchy sweater that had somehow found its way into her closet, but it was time to break up with the old look and let go of the pain.

"God," she prayed, desperately wanting to do the right thing, "I want to love my father, not because he deserves it but because Your Word tells me to honor my mother and father, and I want to honor You by honoring him."

After several months of prayer, a sweet love welled up in Lizbeth as God opened His heavenly treasure chest and exchanged her bitterness for true compassion. God had done the impossible and had extracted the old bitterness, tossing it away forever like an unwanted garment.

"This is crazy," she said with a laugh. "I genuinely love my father!"

Out of the blue, the phone rang: it was her father. After a quick greeting, Lizbeth's newfound compassion spilled into their conversation.

"Dad, I love you."

He was shocked and even apologized for being absent during her childhood. Then he encouraged her for the first time in her

life, saying, "You're a dreamer, and you're going to go far. I'm so proud of you!"

Promising to visit and rejoicing in their reconciliation, her dad hung up the phone, and Lizbeth was overjoyed. God was healing her heart and allowing her to love her dad in a powerful

Every time you smile at someone, it is an action of love, a gift to that person, a beautiful thing.

—Mother Teresa

way. Little did she know that was the last time they would speak. Three months later, she received another phone call informing her that her father had died. Even in the devastation, Lizbeth realized that God had created an opportunity for them to resolve their painful relationship, knowing that the end was near. Her choice to exchange bitterness for grace had enabled the reconciliation to take place before her father left this earth.

Lizbeth continued to work in the fashion industry until she felt God was asking her to lay it down and enter the mission field in Mexico. After our interview, she took me to a home where young women from the red-light district can find refuge from gangs, prostitution, and drug abuse. Lizbeth shared how her work with the women encourages them to make healthy life choices and receive a fresh start as she passes on the hope she found on her own journey.

About a year after our first interview, I reconnected with Lizbeth and was delighted to discover that her passion for beauty was touching lives on an even grander scale. She still loves making women feel beautiful and often has the opportunity to live her dream by working as a stylist for fashion shows in Los Angeles, but her passion to share the beauty of Christ's love has become the heartbeat of her life. She now directs an international ministry called Beauty Arise, which speaks into the lives of young women through a six-week discipleship program and helps them find their identity in Christ. Last I heard, she was on a flight to

Thailand to share this message. Choosing to exchange lies for the truth made all the difference in Lizbeth's world and now enables her to change the world around her.

Photo Shoot

Driving to Ensenada, Mexico, was a crazy adventure. I didn't realize driving to Mexico alone would be difficult until my poor, confused GPS directed me into the wild mountains on a little dirt road for a scenic detour. Thankfully, I somehow arrived at the mission center and my blood pressure returned to normal. We captured Lizbeth's before photos on the dirt road outside the campus. It must have rained recently, because several huge potholes were filled with grimy brown mud. *Perfect for a photo shoot,* I thought. Lizbeth positioned herself on the road, holding

the signs she had made with the words DIRTY, UGLY, and NOT ENOUGH.

Then, after shedding her dark, oversized clothing, Lizbeth donned a bright, fun outfit for the beach. As the sun set, I snapped photos of her newfound freedom as she posed with ropes of pearls on her neck and ocean spray in her face. The beautiful photos represented the glorious exchange in her heart.

My Story

Makeovers were my personal nemesis for a long time, until God changed my perspective. In my late teens and early twenties, my wardrobe consisted of blue jeans, flannel shirts, and T-shirts. My mom was a tomboy, so our dress code was pretty much "no dressing up." When I started speaking publicly in my early twenties, I thought, *I don't want to draw attention to myself, so I'll be humble and keep the focus on God by dressing simply.*

In truth, I was scared. I had never been taught about style, so I would awkwardly stand in a clothing store overwhelmed and completely mystified by so many options. I wanted to dress in a way that communicated dignity, respect, and confident leadership to my audiences, but I was clueless as to how to do it. The other difficulty involved my private belief that ugly was better with God. *If charm is deceitful and beauty vain,* I reasoned, *then perhaps all style and physical beauty are evil.* In my mind, God wasn't interested in the things of this world, so in order to please Him, I shouldn't care about style. So I purchased a dress from a thrift store for my speaking engagements. It looked like a burlap sack.

Slowly, God challenged my thinking, and the Holy Spirit prompted me to start experimenting with beauty. I began to meet godly women who honored their bodies without demeaning their spiritual lives. I realized that my belief that God doesn't care about beauty covered a longing to enjoy life as a woman, but I had been too scared to admit it. In truth, our culture places the beauty bar so high that some of us can never achieve what we think is beautiful, so it is easier not to try, and we cling to a false humility that actually devalues who God created us to be. Part of my freedom was discovering that my value was not defined by outward beauty. At the same time, the beauty of my heart could be celebrated. I learned to enjoy everything God had made me to be, and this included dressing up and learning what looked good on the body He had given me.

The real shocker came when I was hired to direct a documentary about a runway model and decided to act in the film as the lead character. Talk about irony! I bleached my hair blonde, bought some red lipstick, and brought in a wardrobe stylist to create high-fashion outfits. To my shock, I loved it. In fact, being free from the fear of failing enabled me to jump on board with the role and to do it well.

Hopefully, outward beauty will never be my motivation, and I would still preach wearing a burlap sack if God asked me to, but it is fun to embrace beauty in the many forms God has given us to enjoy.

God's Story (Zech. 3)

Makeovers happen in heaven—no joke. We get a glimpse of one divine stylist session in the writings of Zechariah, the prophet who saw a vision about five hundred years before Jesus was born on earth. Zechariah 3 offers a fascinating look at how God desires to give us a fresh look and release our destiny. I have used a little artistic license to make the story come alive.

Joshua stood in the courtroom, silent and afraid. It was a heavenly judgment room of sorts, a vast meeting hall where the King of Kings sat upon the judgment seat and pondered a case that had been brought before Him. Radiant angelic beings stood at attention, watching the proceedings that took place before the heavenly throne. Joshua knew he was on trial, and not just him but the entire Israelite city where he lived. Jerusalem had rebelled against God and had been horrendously defeated by her enemies as a result. Joshua saw no hope for a future unless God moved on his behalf.

Next to Joshua, Satan stood as the prosecutor, heaping blame and accusations against him with a vengeance. The list of allegations was long and mercilessly throbbed in Joshua's ears, but he had no defense.

"Jerusalem has sinned," hissed the devil, making a case before the Judge. "You cannot ignore their rebellion. And this man," he turned toward Joshua and, moving close to his right side, said, "is not fit to lead a nation. Have you seen what he's done? Look, even his clothes describe where he's been," he finished with disgust.

Joshua looked at his clothes, which were filthy and torn. Nothing could be hidden here before the throne, and Joshua knew that the dirt from his difficult road still clung to his robes. The call on his life was strong, and he knew that God had chosen him to help rebuild his city and place of worship, but leadership seemed impossible. Everyone knew what a failure he was, especially God. Joshua miserably wished he could disappear.

Suddenly, the Lord spoke with authority. The gavel fell, and thundering tones echoed that immediately silenced the sneers of the prosecutor. "I reject your accusations, Satan. I have decided to be merciful to Jerusalem. I have decreed mercy to Joshua and his nation, and I have chosen them for My purpose; they are like a burning stick pulled out of the fire."

Astonished, Joshua raised his head just in time to see his enemy wince with a defeated snarl and angrily storm out of the room. Looking at the Judge, he saw determined compassion and mercy filling His eyes. Gesturing toward a heavenly being and nodding toward Joshua, the Judge said, "Remove his filthy clothing."

Angels surrounded Joshua, peeling off layers of thickly matted, soiled material. As they removed the dirty robes, Joshua watched every bit of his past history being erased. The old was gone, never to be seen again.

"See," the Lord said tenderly, "I have taken away your sin, and I am giving you fresh, new clothing to wear."

Joshua raised his head, tears streaming down his face as the angels dressed him in a new wardrobe. Looking closer, he realized these were not just any clothes; they were the clothes of the high priest. God had not just removed his sin; He was clothing him in the destiny and calling Joshua had dreamed of. Joshua was being prepared to lead his people in worship and restoration and to bring healing to a land destroyed by the enemy.

"Joshua!" the Lord called to him, earnestly looking into his eyes and entrusting him with a new assignment. "If you follow the paths I set for you and do all I tell you to do, then I will put you in charge of My temple, to keep it holy, and I will let you walk in and out of My presence with these angels." His voice became filled with anticipation and excitement as He spoke of future plans. "Listen to Me, Joshua. You and the priests are illustrations of the good things to come." He began to talk about the Savior who would come to earth. This man would silence the accuser for all who followed God and would bring peace with God by granting

121

everyone robes clean and white. Peace would finally reign, and the accuser would be defeated.

The heavenly vision ceased. Only the prophet had seen what had happened in heaven, and with a trembling hand, he wrote it down to be preserved for generations until Christ would come, bringing fine linen clean and white for all those who would choose to follow Him.

∽∾

Today we don't have to go to heaven to get a makeover. We can choose it today because Christ bought it for us, purchasing righteousness on the cross and silencing the accuser on our behalf. When we receive God's special gift of grace and a new identity, then we can toss out the lies placed on our lives. God's wardrobe is clean and stunningly beautiful and perfectly fits His children. No longer are we required to wear the filthy robes of our past or listen to the accuser's lies. We are daughters of the great King, and He gives us a brand-new wardrobe for the heart.

True Beauty Tip

Romans 13:14 says, "But put on the Lord Jesus Christ, and make no provision for the flesh, to fulfill its lusts." In the Greek language, "put on" literally means "to sink into a garment, array, clothe with, put on." Christ invites us to wear His truth on our hearts like a beautiful garment. He invites us to put on His love and presence every day. By doing this, we will be able to avoid filthy garments and doing things in our own strength. Let's choose to make the great exchange and trust our heavenly Stylist to give us His best.

Questions for Reflection

1. If I gave you a piece of cardboard and a marker, what words would you write for your before picture? Why?

2. Can you recognize where those lies came from?

3. What is the truth about God's love?

4. In what ways can you "put on Christ" and choose to believe His heart for you?

eight

Beautiful Warrior

I am not afraid. . . . I was born to do this.
—Joan of Arc

Every day we step into a war zone where a critical battle threatens our destiny as women of God. On this battlefield of the mind, an evil nemesis plots our demise and plans every possible attack to undermine God's love and plan for our lives. The bullets may vary in size, but the lies of rejection, fear, and doubt that whiz past us every day all have the same purpose: to keep us from our Father's love, steal our freedom, and destroy our joy. Now and then we meet a woman who stands firm, wages war against the foe, and wins such a great victory that we also pick up our gleaming swords and declare, "If she can do it, so can I!" I believe that call to greatness lives in each of our hearts, waiting for us to embrace this warrior woman who plants her feet and refuses to surrender to anything less than the truth of who God calls her to be.

I met one of these inspiring women while visiting Israel, a nation torn by war and held together by sheer determination. As Oriel walked across the old stone courtyard in Jerusalem, she carried the persona of a soldier whose presence should not be taken lightly. This young woman in her midtwenties and of slight build had straight brunette hair that fell below her shoulders and framed large, thoughtful blue eyes filled with calm courage. *This young woman has fought for her identity*, I sensed, *and she has won.* Above the noisy street traffic inside the walls of the Old City, we talked about her childhood move to Israel from the United States and how her insecurities grew after she arrived in Jerusalem. It seemed that the moment her family moved to the Middle East, the mounting battle for her identity turned into a full-blown war.

"It has to be understood like this," she stated in precise, definitive English. "When I was in the States, I wasn't a threat to the devil. The moment I came to Israel, all hell broke loose in my life."

"Explain this to me," I said, intrigued. "What do you believe frightened the forces of darkness?"

"A person who loves is unstoppable," she said, "and I had made a decision to love God and love all people. I believe that the enemy thought, *If this girl understands God's love and her calling and decides to obey God, she's a threat.* Sometimes when we move into the place we're supposed to be, things become difficult because the enemy knows that we're capable of much good."

Oriel's Story

Oriel came from a line of valiant warriors who fought for both their identity and their lives. During the late 1930s and early

1940s, her great-grandparents lived through the horror of the Holocaust in Europe. The family hid from the Nazis in their neighbors' basement, and Oriel's grandmother saw only basement walls for the first five years of her life. Without daylight or ever seeing her reflection, the child thought she was blonde and blue-eyed until she saw a mirror for the first time. Shocked by her brown hair and eyes, Oriel's grandmother was horrified and decided she was ugly, since she didn't look anything like the other European children. She even tried to commit suicide on the boat to Israel when the family moved after the war. Like many other Jewish survivors of World War II, Oriel's family sank their roots deeply into the soil of their new homeland, the budding nation of Israel, and felt relieved to be safe from racial genocide. With a stubbornness that defied their enemies, they vowed to heal from past abuse and rebuild their identity as a nation and a people.

As the years of oppression retreated into the past, a piece of the aftermath refused to be buried. Just as Oriel's grandmother had been trapped in a basement and left to deal with her shaken identity, Oriel would relive that strange fate generations later. She would both fight the same battles and carry the warrior spirit to overcome and establish her identity as a child of God. The road would not be easy, but she would plunge deeper than most people dare to go in their quest for beauty, and she would find real answers for those of us who walk toward our own destiny as a beautiful warrior.

Oriel grew up in Texas with spacious ranches, few neighbors, and plenty of Southern hospitality. Her parents had met in Israel and had decided to move to the United States, where they started a family and raised their children with the knowledge of God. With childlike simplicity, Oriel always talked to God, and she remembers Him talking to her. Even her simple times of play held a sweet devotion and spiritual connection. She knew she had His attention, and many times He answered her prayers, but there was one problem she couldn't seem to resolve: she desperately wanted to be beautiful.

For as long as she could remember, Oriel felt horribly ugly. She felt too pale and too skinny, her skin was easily irritated, her nose was too big, her ears stuck out . . . there wasn't one thing she loved about her body. Ugliness followed her like a rabid dog she couldn't shake, crushing every shred of self-worth and denying her right to confidence. Staring at herself in the mirror, she sometimes fell into a panic attack as she tried to scratch "the ugly off her skin," all the while begging God to make her beautiful. As she fell asleep every night, she asked God to fix everything by the next morning, but He seemed deaf to her prayers. *Why doesn't God make me beautiful? Is that too hard for Him?* she wondered. *Why did He make me ugly? Am I cursed?*

Even among the kind community in Texas, her fears felt confirmed. At church one day, Oriel's mother was chatting with a friend and introduced the shy girl. The other woman gasped. "What is *that?* She looks like a skeleton. Don't you feed her?"

Shocked, her mother was too surprised to say anything in defense, and Oriel turned crimson with embarrassment. *My mother is not defending me, so these accusations must be true,* she surmised, wanting to crawl into a hole.

She began to fear blushing almost as much as she feared her mother, a very practical, no-nonsense Jewish woman who had been raised in war-torn Israel and didn't quite understand her daughter's sensitivities. When Oriel was nine, the family decided to move back to Jerusalem, so Oriel began school in the new country before she even learned the Hebrew language. Culture

shock shifted her struggle to a new battlefield with Israeli students who were boisterous, strong-willed, and often critical of the kind, gentle girl with Southern manners. *This is a zoo,* she thought, but she didn't know if she was the animal or they were.

Even though bullying was constant at school, kindness for others filled Oriel's heart like a little fire that refused to be stomped out, and she continued to reach out with love to the students around her. In response, the belittling grew even worse, and she felt that even her small acts of goodness went unappreciated. Being the "nice girl" had its perks: teachers often paired her with new students who needed a helping hand, but soon they realized she was not popular with her peers and left her for other friends. Several times she was told by students, "You're not beautiful enough to be my friend."

Like an outdated doll set aside for a brighter, shinier toy, Oriel felt she was only filling up space until a peer found someone better. The twin fiends of rejection and self-hatred paraded themselves around her soul, mocking her attempts at friendship and feeding her shyness. Even if she was kind and loving, no one seemed to care, so she began to feel that goodness didn't matter either.

Boys were another difficulty. She knew that none of them liked her, so when one approached her at recess, she was skeptical.

"You know, you're really beautiful," he said.

With graciousness, she was about to receive the compliment, but suddenly she stopped and wondered if he was being earnest. *Why would he tell me I'm beautiful?* she wondered, so she asked him to repeat himself. At her response, the boy shuffled his feet with embarrassment, then turned without a word, walked away, and handed money to his friend: he had lost the bet to make the ugly girl believe she was beautiful and had to pay up. A strange pit filled Oriel's stomach. Instead of congratulating herself on discerning a false motive, a thought of horror invaded her heart. *Someone just made money off my ugliness,* she thought, choking back a sob. *I must not be worth anything at all.*

Adding to her woes was the unstable political situation. The family had arrived in Israel just prior to the intifada, a violent Palestinian uprising in which random acts of terror pummeled the city of Jerusalem. Shootings, bombs, and lynchings took the lives of three thousand Palestinians and one thousand Israelis. Watching TV one day, Oriel was horrified to see that a pizza parlor she had just visited had become the site of a suicide bombing.

She scanned the scene, noting that the table she had recently eaten pizza at was now covered in blood. *That could have been me on the floor,* she thought in shock. The hostile environment fed her insecurity, and she couldn't understand why everyone in the world seemed to hate her country and the Jewish people. She was in a war simply by being alive.

With hostility swirling around her, Oriel began to withdraw in humiliation. When severe acne plagued her skin and her thin body didn't develop as fast as those of her teenage classmates, she felt like a monster unable to cope with the social pressures. Lashing out at her Creator, she prayed, "God, why are You rejecting me? I love You so much, but why didn't You love me enough to make me beautiful, or at least normal? You must hate me too."

Locking her door, she shut herself off from the world in her basement bedroom. Panic attacks, insomnia, and self-harm took over her life. Dark nightmares invaded her sleep. She attempted suicide, but the pills only made her sick. Constant arguments with her parents caused her to retreat deeper into her world. For a year and a half, she stayed at home, stubbornly refusing to leave her room. After she missed so much school without a reasonable excuse, social workers threatened to take her to a psychiatric ward.

In the middle of the battle for her sanity, a tiny flame of love still fought for survival in her heart: no matter what happened, Oriel couldn't stop loving God. She couldn't understand why He had made her ugly, and she couldn't feel His love in return—in fact, she felt that He too had overlooked her efforts of goodness—but she remembered her childhood conversations and knew He was real. In her private torment, she still reached out to Him in prayer, even though she believed He hated her and rejected the love she wanted to give.

Oriel's brother tenaciously pursued her freedom, pleading for hours with his little sister and trying to find ways to master the fear. When he couldn't convince her that she was beautiful, he made a paper mask so she wouldn't have to show her face in front of people, since she was terrified of blushing. When social workers determined to check her into a hospital without her consent, he sat down on her bed for one more chat. That day, when she had no place left to run, her brother found the way to reach her heart.

"Oriel, if you say that you love God and believe in Him, then you have to believe that He is Who He says He is—and He is love."

Oriel sat up, shocked. Feeling rejected by those who wouldn't receive her love was the greatest pain she had ever known. Suddenly, she was faced with a question she had never thought of before. *Am I rejecting God by refusing to believe that He loves me?* The wheels turned in her head as she remembered the pain she felt when peers rejected the love she offered them. *If God cannot lie, and He says that He loves me, then it must be true. If everything else in my life screams that He doesn't, all else must be untrue, because God cannot lie.*

Stubbornness rose up within her, and this time she determined to fight for love at all costs. She decided that she wasn't going to reject God's love the way that friends and students had tossed hers aside.

"I love You, so I'm going to fight for the joy of loving You," she vowed to God. "Even if I don't feel it, I'm going to believe that You love me too. So I'm going to leave this room to get help even if it kills me."

At the hospital, she began to receive treatment and even met new friends who followed Christ and encouraged her faith. Nothing came easily, since her healing involved the process of fighting off lies about God, herself, and what others thought, until her mind began to break free. The divine makeover had begun, as the cries of her heart were heard and answered through the life-giving hands of those around her.

One day she read a Scripture verse that shook the core of her soul, bringing up a thought she had never considered before. Jesus said, "If the world hates you, you know that it hated Me before it hated you" (John 15:18). Oriel realized that Christ had also experienced intense hatred, but His identity was never at stake, nor did it define how He felt about Himself or His Father. Instead, He took the rejection and shame willingly so that the world might have a picture of how far God would go to show His love. He told the disciples, "I'm going to suffer for your sake. I'm going to be

mocked and spat on by people I love. This is going to hurt . . . but I'm going to do this for you. You need to see how much I'm willing to love you." During every moment of Christ's sacrifice—the kiss of a betrayer, abandonment by His close friends, the beating and brutal crucifixion—Jesus was willing to suffer if the end result was that people could recognize the Father's love.

> *I have found the paradox, that if you love until it hurts, there can be no more hurt, only more love.*
>
> —Mother Teresa

Oriel was shocked, realizing for the first time that love is costly yet completely worth the price, even if people don't understand in the moment. Just because her small acts of goodness went unnoticed by her classmates didn't mean her love was not valuable to God. In fact, if her kindness was not immediately rewarded, she could persevere and choose to show it anyway, recognizing that love was more powerful than the crude behavior of others. Love was worth fighting and even suffering for so that others might one day come to know it. *True beauty*, she realized, *requires a passion to fight for love.*

"You know what," she whispered to God, "if being with You means being rejected, then I don't mind. If this is the price for love, I'll pay it."

Suddenly, the windows of her soul were thrown open and light streamed in, blindingly sweet and in stark contrast to the black despair she had known for so long. Rejection was no longer her identity. Christ was despised and rejected, yet He chose to love anyway, and she could do the same. With this revelation, she was finally free. The war was not over and there would be more battles

ahead, but the tide had turned and victory was in sight. Unafraid of the future, this beautiful warrior was ready to stand her ground and fight for her identity and the love she had to offer. The evil nemesis of rejection had lost, and true beauty had won.

When I interviewed Oriel, she was working at a church in the heart of Jerusalem and had helped coordinate a house of prayer for people of many nations. I visited the prayer tower on the twentieth floor of a high-rise where people can spend time in worship and prayer. From the window, I caught a bird's-eye view of the city. It was quite the opposite of Oriel's basement bedroom and a powerful picture of where Christ can lead us when we fight for freedom.

135

Photo Shoot

For Oriel's before photos, I wanted to capture the idea of feeling alone in a crowd, so we stepped into a narrow street in Jerusalem. As crowds of people surged past her, Oriel stood with torn cardboard scraps labeled with her past insecurities: UNLOVED, MONSTROUS, and REJECTED. One woman on the street saw her holding the sign UNLOVED and interrupted our shoot. "That's not true!" she argued. "You are loved!"

Oriel laughed, explaining to her that it was just for a photo, before getting back into character and attempting to look depressed again. I wondered how many times we would encourage one another if our struggles were always written on cardboard signs.

For her after photos, Oriel wore a stylish outfit, and I curled her hair. We headed down the Old City's labyrinth of streets and tunnels, stopping by the Church of the Holy Sepulchre, one of the possible locations of Christ's empty tomb. Posing her against curiously carved stones, I shot photos of this gorgeous young woman. This time she held signs that read AT PEACE and ALIVE. Her radiant smile told the story—true love is real! We can fight against the lies and overcome, being free to give and receive love.

My Story

Shortly after interviewing Oriel, I hopped on a plane to visit a French cathedral where another young warrior named Joan of Arc experienced a great victory. She offers us another glimpse of how God raises up people to be soldiers who least expect it.

Raised as a quiet country girl in France, Joan was only thirteen years old when she began to have visions and heavenly encounters. Her nation was in chaos, with murders, kidnappings, and assassinations running rampant in the royal monarchy and plagues and illness sweeping through the population. Enemy armies had captured major cities, and they were just about to pounce on the capital, Orléans. No one expected the French to thwart the attack, but the French people clung to several ancient prophecies that spoke of a female warrior who would rescue the nation.

"A virgin from the borders of Lorraine will work miracles, and France will be restored," they promised.

Standing in her father's garden one day, a girl from Lorraine named Joan had a vision of heavenly beings who brought her a message. "Drive out the English armies and bring the new king to Reims for his coronation!" they charged her.

Accounts tell us that Joan cried when the messengers left, not from fear but because the heavenly beings were so beautiful. She spent much time in the church, praying to Christ and waiting for directions. Surely, voices of doubt raised objections to the thought of obeying God's call. The obstacles were huge and rejection was almost certain: she was young, a woman, and illiterate, and she had never been trained for war. Yet moved by the beauty of heaven and her love for Christ, she decided to take the plunge. Although women rarely left their villages, Joan journeyed to a nearby town to ask the army commander for a garrison of troops so she could go to war.

"I must be at the king's side," she confided. "There is no help for the kingdom if not from me. Although I would rather have remained spinning [wool] at my mother's side, yet I must go and do this thing, for my Lord wills that it is so."*

*Régine Pernoud, *Joan of Arc* (New York: St. Martins Griffin, 1999), 35.

Against all odds, Joan received her troops and won a battle. Her biggest weapon was her banner, which she declared was "forty times better than a sword," and it encouraged the men to fight valiantly. She spearheaded the fight for freedom, and multiple battles were won. Strangely enough, Joan's biggest goal was not for herself but for another: the new king could be crowned only at the cathedral at Reims, the religious capital of France, which was cut off from the French by invaders. Joan's victories cut a swath through the enemy armies so that the gates of Reims could open and the joyous coronation of King Charles could take place.

Joan died at the tender age of nineteen, but in that short time, she lived more fully than many people do in a lifetime. Moved by heaven and the call of her Master, she abandoned the obvious path and chose to pioneer a lonely road for the sake of love and beauty. As a result, she stands tall as one who overcame the giants of doubt and fulfilled her destiny.

While standing at that cathedral in Reims, I observed Joan's statue in the shadow of the huge church and political buildings. She looked so small, just a petite figure against an army of intimidating foes. Suddenly, my heart swelled with courage, and I thought, *If she can do it, so can I!* Maybe leaving home and riding into battle isn't our price tag for loving God, but we still encounter the twisted face of rejection in other ways. Maybe rejection raises its head when we think about investing extra time into someone we care about or stepping out in a new dream. The thoughts *You won't succeed, People won't care,* and *It doesn't matter anyway* parade through our minds, challenging us to agree with the lies and speak them into being. No matter how big or small our challenge, we wage war every day to determine whether we will overcome rejection and step into God's call on our lives.

God's Story (John 16:33; 1 John 4:4, 18)

Muted light flickered through the window, flushing the simple wooden desk below with a soft glow. Bending low over the parchment, the aged apostle gently touched its rough surface with a reed dipped in ink. His fingers were wrinkled with age, and burns scarred his body; his skin bore marks of torture, but his words were clear and profound. He recalled the words that Jesus had spoken just before His crucifixion.

> These things I have spoken to you, that in Me you may have peace. In the world you will have tribulation; but be of good cheer, I have overcome the world.

John, the disciple closest to Jesus, briefly lifted the reed and recalled the devastating moments when the Master was arrested, mocked, spit upon, beaten, and paraded through the street on public display like a criminal. He was rejected by the religious leaders of the day and found innocent yet condemned to die by the civil authorities. Even the common people called for His death. John recalled all these scenes for just a moment, pondering how the world had thrown its worst blows at his Friend. *Yet,* he mused with certainty, *God's perspective trumps them all.* After the brutal crucifixion, Christ had risen from the dead, proving that God has the final say in regard to His children. The end was only the beginning of a brand-new era.

Setting aside his first parchment, John picked up a letter he was writing to the church he had founded. He wanted to remind them that they too were overcomers, because Christ lived within them. With determined strokes, he wrote, "You are of God, little children, and have overcome them, because He who is in you is greater than he who is in the world."

The aged man recalled moments when large crowds had misunderstood his call to follow the Master. Over the years, he too had endured beatings, imprisonments, and even the Roman punishment of being boiled in hot oil in an attempt to deter his faith. Yet the same tenacious love still beat in his chest, untamed and wild with the joyous heartbeat of Christ. This love was so reckless that it could not be stopped by anything in this world. "There is no fear in love; but perfect love casts out fear, because fear involves torment." *No fear*, thought John with a smile. Even in the face of difficulty, the powerful love of Christ blots it out and gives us the power to love others. We are the victors, as long as we love as He did.

True Beauty Tip

Overcoming rejection and choosing love make a woman beautiful. We have all had people think the worst of us, and it is easy to accept critical remarks and believe them. However, there is a better way. Unwrapping the lies that mesh themselves in our thoughts and hold us captive requires time and effort, but with God's help, we can live free as warriors of the King.

Questions for Reflection

1. How have you experienced rejection?
2. Do you see rejection as an assault on your character or an opportunity to show God's love?
3. What are some ways you can overcome rejection and step into God's call on your life?
4. Does it encourage you to know that God takes note of every time you choose to love whether others applaud it or not? Explain.

nine

Beautiful Vulnerability

*I was going to stop pretending that just because we were in
ministry we were perfect. I was tired of wearing the mask of
ministry, and knew that I needed to start living the life.*

—Anna Aquino

It was glory hour—that moment when the setting sun turns everything golden just before dusk. This muted light cast a delightful
hue on our fairy tale–themed film shoot in which fresh flowers
graced an outdoor table set with fine china, white linen, bright
fruit, and loaves of French bread. Candles softly flickered in the
twilight, and the romantic garden banquet was ready for guests.
My muse Charla wore a form-fitting, black satin dress that just
barely brushed the ground, and her dark hair was swept up into
a classic updo. Entering the garden, she walked with elegant steps
toward the feast and slid into a chair. Her place setting was marked
by a name card penned with a single word: BELOVED.

That evening I was shooting a music video for our makeover girl's original song that perfectly accompanied her story, and we had staged the table scene to fit her lyrics:

Then You take me
To Your table
I am wanted
I'm invited
And Your banner over me
Is love
It's a perfect love
A never-ending love story

Although the scene looked like the perfect fantasy, the story behind this banquet was more like a dramatic mystery than a fairy tale. In our interview earlier that day, Charla had dared to strip off every pretense and reveal the secrets of her heart. For years, she had remained hidden behind a mask painted with a smiling face she wished was real, but it only disguised a throbbing pain. Beneath the stoic smile lay dark secrets and a mysterious grief. Carefully removing the layers and dislodging the truth had been a long journey, but slowly a reckoning had come, and each hint of freedom was sweet to her soul. Today her smile is broad and real, and she helps us discover ways we can remove our masks and be vulnerable enough to expose our true hearts.

Charla's Story

Once upon a time, a little girl named Charla loved to sing and make music with all her heart. Her father was the worship leader of their local church, and her parents and siblings traveled the local church circuit singing gospel hymns as a family band. Charla joined the family in song at the age of three and continued sing-ing for the next twelve years, adding her soft voice to the band. Piling into the car, they drove to little country chapels, belting out choruses and love songs with swelling harmonies that brought smiles to those in the audience. "Just look at this godly family!" people marveled as they observed the group dressed in their cute, matching outfits. But behind the picture-perfect family was another story.

Charla knew the family secret: her father was prone to fly into fits of rage that placed the entire family in danger. Without rea-son, he would angrily threaten the children, and Charla became terrified that she might die if she so much as spilled her milk. Road rage was also a common occurrence, like the day twelve-year-old Charla watched her father aggressively dodge traffic while pursuing another car as both drivers yelled and wove across the highway. The other driver finally pulled over, and Charla remem-bers a large, muscular man covered in tattoos beating on the windows as her father taunted the stranger. Cowering in the front seat, her mother held the terrified girl and tried to cover her eyes and ears so the child wouldn't see or hear her father's rage, but the scene burned into Charla's mind. Screaming in her head was the silent cry, *This is so wrong! How can we say we serve God but live such a lie when no one is watching?*

At church, an angry God was painted in her childhood mind. She became terrified of going to hell, so she said a simple sin-ner's prayer in an attempt to escape the fate of unbelievers. However, the truth of her heavenly Father's love never impacted her heart, and she scrambled to cope with the example of her earthly father, who demanded perfection yet refused to emotion-ally connect with his daughter. While she knew the answer to every Sunday school question, Charla was stubbornly angry with the contradiction between church life and home life, and her feeble attempt at Christianity became a mask of pasted-on smiles to cover the hurt inside.

On her first high school date, a young man wanted to touch Charla intimately, and she quickly refused. Instead of respecting her wishes, the boy instantly broke off the relationship. Charla felt the sting of rejection slap her soul, shattering a fragile heart that was so desperate for a man's love. She realized that a new form of male relationship was available to her, but it came with a costly price tag. *If this is what it takes to win a man's affection,* she vowed, *I'll never say no again.* From that point on, she did whatever was required to keep a relationship with a boy alive, even if it meant giving her body away. At first, her mind buzzed with excitement. *These guys think I'm beautiful—it's awesome!* But then the breakups left her desperately lonely, and pretty soon she was dependent on drugs and alcohol to numb her bleeding heart.

No one knew that the worship leader's daughter was living out her pain this way. As a gymnast and a cheerleader, Charla was so tightly glued to her mask that it was almost impossible for the truth to penetrate her soul . . . until the first shock of reality splashed over her like an icy bucket of spring water. Her mom had a dream that her daughter, at sixteen years of age, was pregnant. Charla swore it wasn't true, but her mother bought a pregnancy test, and the positive result sent shock waves through them both. The mask was wearing thin, and this time it wasn't able to cover the brokenness beneath.

Charla was numb and terrified of carrying a child. She began exercising more and eating less, secretly hoping the child inside her would naturally disappear, but nothing changed. Her mom and boyfriend started making plans: to save face in religious

circles and fearing their lives would be at stake if her father found out, they decided that Charla should quietly deal with the situation by having an abortion. They drove her to the local clinic and sat in the waiting room during the procedure. Automatically, Charla obeyed, steeling herself as the nurse began to read off a list of possible side effects of the operation: "Extensive bleeding, fever, abdominal pain, depression . . ."

Fear began to grip the teenager, and she slipped into the waiting room to whisper a plea for a release to her mother.

"We're already here," came the answer. "You have to go through with it."

A familiar hardness crept over Charla's emotions. *Suck it up. You've dealt with hard things before, so let's just get this over with,* she told herself through gritted teeth as she slipped back into the surgery room and signed the papers for the operation.

Lying on the table during the procedure, Charla felt her head spin. As her tiny child was pulled from her womb, a silent scream ripped through her soul. She sensed heaven weeping, as if she was in the middle of a sacred tragedy in which innocence was lost and the promise of a new life was shattered. Crying filled the room outside, where women lay on cots after their abortions until the bleeding stopped, and she could hear one woman openly sobbing. Soon Charla lay on a cot too, and strange new emotions stampeded through her sixteen-year-old soul.

"Abortion," she confided, years after that moment, "not only kills the child but also puts a gun to the natural mothering instinct—the mama bear—inside a woman. I was wrecked by emotions: I, the mother, had willingly killed my child. I couldn't grieve as a mother for the loss of my child, nor could I take responsibility for the murder, because I was too ashamed and horrified by what I had done. The natural need to grieve over the loss of life was stolen from me because I was the perpetrator of this crime. There was nothing to do but try to stuff the grief inside."

Her mom tried to ease the pain by offering to take her to get ice cream, but Charla was so emotionally wrecked that they drove to her grandmother's house instead and told the family she was sick. Charla sat with her boyfriend in the spare bedroom, doubled over in pain. Anger welled up in her, and she stormed, "I'm being forced to walk around and pretend that I'm not a mother who just lost a child!" When she finally fell into a troubled sleep, a lie was pressed into her mind: *You're worthless and shameful.*

In a weird twist of fate, some of Charla's immoral behavior was exposed to her high school classmates, and she became the talk of the town. They vandalized her house and held crude signs while she performed as a cheerleader. When she appealed to the school principal, he refused to get involved. The boys made up stories, and the girls hated her, except for a handful of Christian friends from youth group.

Charla had lost every shred of self-respect. Tearfully, she picked up her Bible and began trying to find some meaning to life. The Psalms gripped the teenage girl as she read the ancient text:

> O Lord, how many are my foes!
>   Many are rising against me;
> many are saying of my soul,
>   "There is no salvation for him in God." Selah
> But you, O Lord, are a shield about me,
>   my glory, and the lifter of my head. (Ps. 3:1–3 ESV)

This part of the Bible made sense to her. *King David had enemies,* she thought, *and God helped him survive. I have enemies too, so maybe God can help me.* Charla discovered that the psalmists expressed deep, intense emotions to God, and they never hid from their anger, regret, or shame. Instead, King David and others discovered how tangibly the love of God met them when their masks were removed and their true hearts were exposed. The Scriptures became Charla's life source, a way to find comfort when her security was lacking.

One day Charla slipped into her country church and listened to a guest preacher who picked up a guitar and began to sing about Jesus. A strange emotion gripped her, and suddenly the Spirit of God began to make the gospel story real to her. "For God so loved the world . . ." Charla chewed on every word and slipped her own name into the well-worn verse. "For God so loved Charla, that He sent His only begotten Son." Tears began to stream down her face as waves of conviction and grace flooded her heart. *I'm a sinner,* she realized, *but God is offering hope, not punishment.* God was not brushing her pain under the rug; instead, He was offering to save her from the shame she desperately tried to hide. *Whosoever believes on Him has everlasting life,* she pondered, marveling at the words. In that moment, she was handed an open invitation to grace in which the heartfelt conviction of sin was real and the call to receive Christ's forgiveness was extended. She realized that God wanted her to leave the fake, smiling mask in the pew and come running into His arms.

Bawling, Charla bolted to the altar. Raw emotion spilled out as she grabbed hold of this fresh concept of grace with all her might. The church leaders weren't quite sure how to handle this response from the music minister's daughter, so they dubbed it "a rededication to Christ," but in her heart, Charla knew that this was the moment of her true salvation. The change was immediate as the simple power of the gospel exploded in her life. God's Word spoke to her like never before, and many of her destructive life patterns simply ceased to exist. Breathing life into her soul like CPR from heaven, this newfound grace brought fresh purpose as she repositioned her life around the love of God.

Over ten years after her abortion experience, Charla's life held an entirely new significance. She became passionate about

> *To what greater inspiration and counsel can we turn than to the imperishable truth to be found in this treasure house, the Bible?*
>
> —Queen Elizabeth II

loving and fighting for fragile life, whether that meant working with children in a church ministry, traveling to Nigeria to fight against sex trafficking, or using her degree in dentistry to care for the elderly and frail at a nursing home.

"Life is a treasure," she said, "and I'm in love with the raw beauty of every living soul."

However, one door to her past stayed locked, and she determined that no one was going to pry their way in. While she had received the forgiveness of Christ for the abortion, she had never grieved the loss of her child. Friends encouraged her to attend

151

a postabortion class, and she agreed, promising herself, *I'm not going to get emotional like the other women.* But instead of breezing through the class, Charla discovered a vault of emotions she had never dared to address. A soft awakening crept over her heart as she realized that she could receive the license to grieve. She could name her child, be thankful for its life in the womb, and have a second chance to honor its memory.

More healing came on Mother's Day, when Charla visited her mom on the family homestead. Her parents had finally divorced, and her mom had married a man who truly loved and adored her, bringing a healthy father figure into the family. In the safety of this environment, Charla decided to reach out to her mother. As they sat on the back porch swing, Charla confided the depth of her journey and the pain her abortion had caused. Mother and daughter wept in each other's arms and prayed, remembering the past and asking God if there was anything they could do to bind up the old wound.

"Every year at Thanksgiving dinner," Charla confided with tears, "I look across the family table and remember my child who is supposed to be here. I want my baby to be remembered by my family in a tangible way."

In the backyard grew some young trees that Charla's mother had planted, one for each of her grandchildren. As they swayed in the breeze, a new idea entered Charla's mind.

"I want a tree," she requested. "When the family gathers for holidays, I want my baby represented on this property."

The next day Charla's mother and stepfather drove her to the nursery to choose a plant, and together they dug a hole and firmly embedded the roots of a young olive tree into the homestead soil. A sense of completion filled Charla as she realized that, just like the olives from her tree needed to be crushed to release their rich oil inside, God had used the deep brokenness in her life to release a compassion for others through her. In the past, she had used a smiling mask to hide her brokenness, but God wanted to take the very pain she despised and bring about great beauty. Embracing the Healer, she had become beautifully vulnerable and whole in the arms of her Lord.

Photo Shoot

I snapped Charla's before photos in a forest full of brambles and thorns, where she wrote on a gilded mirror the words of her past: GUILTY and GRIEVING MOTHER. Over her shoulder hung a bag that held jeweled necklaces and brooches, stunning symbols of the treasure she carried. Haphazardly, she pulled the pieces from the bag, dropping them on the forest floor and losing them in piles of dead leaves and branches. This represented how we sometimes carelessly toss aside the treasure God entrusts us with.

I took her after photos at a banquet table, where a feast had been prepared for this woman who was so valuable to the King of Kings. On the table, nestled between chalices and fine china, were the jewels that had been lost. Strings of pearls, sparkling rings, and lavish brooches—every precious piece had been restored, and they shone as she lifted them to the candlelight. God loves to restore our joy, beauty, and ability to love, enabling us to live without fear.

My Story

Vulnerability can be embraced in many ways, and I have dubbed it "beautifully bare." Call me crazy, but I love to walk around barefoot. In warm weather, I am blissfully happy when my naked feet are soaking up the sun. I've been known to kick off my shoes and stand on a grassy cliff in Ireland (even after a warning about stinging nettles) just to feel the fresh dirt on my toes. Slipping my dry feet into a cool stream in the summertime gives me the same thrill, and I definitely have to go barefoot on the beach. There is something wonderful about stripping off footwear just to press my toes into something natural and alive, with nothing between me and the warm earth.

I think we experience a similar joy each time we share a deep conversation with a friend. Our hearts "go barefoot" as we push back protective layers we often wear and honestly share our joys and struggles. Only then can we fully experience the touch of compassion, encouragement, and prayer. We can't live in this vulnerable state all the time, just like a person can't constantly go barefoot, but hearts of kindness are always a safe place to "kick off our shoes" and be real.

Whether or not we have a best friend, Christ welcomes us to come boldly to Him and unveil our true hearts. He sees through every mask and notices the hiding places we are so quick to run to. In our quiet times of prayer, He always offers a safe place for us to express our true selves. We can always be vulnerable and safe in His embrace.

God's Story (Luke 7:36–50)

A heavy fragrance of roasted meat and rosemary filled the air as servants hastily attended to last-minute preparations for the guests. Colorful pillows lined the floor where weary travelers could rest, while the host, Simon the Pharisee, scanned the room to assure himself that all was in order.

"Sir," said one of his servants respectfully, "shall I prepare water to wash your guests' feet and perfumed oil to refresh them? They will be weary after walking many miles today."

The master of the house frowned, creasing his eyebrows as he pondered his guests. *I hardly believe that a motley bunch of fishermen and tax collectors could amount to much,* he reasoned silently, pursing his lips. *Their leader from Galilee is probably uneducated and wouldn't value my expensive ointment anyway.*

"They approach, sir." The servant's comment broke Simon's inner surmising. "Shall we bring water?"

"No, no," he responded impatiently. "Just seat them and bring the food."

Uncertainly, the servant bowed and moved to welcome the guests.

Jesus, the group's leader, carried the gracious, commanding presence of a king, even though He dressed simply and was surrounded by men who tended to be a bit loud and rambunctious. His disciples were famished, and they eagerly settled into the cushions and reached for the bread prepared on their behalf. Jesus greeted His host kindly, noticing the lack of the traditional foot washing and ointment but saying nothing.

"Jesus, we are greatly honored to have You." The Pharisee began a flowery speech, gesturing to his servants to bring in the rest of the food. "My house is blessed that You have set foot on my soil. We have heard of Your great deeds, so You must enlighten us to the things of God!" He laughed, adding a slight, condescending nod toward the young teacher. Before he could continue, a slight rustle from the back of the room caught everyone's attention, and every head turned toward the sound.

It was a woman, veiled from head to toe in a manner that shocked the men: they immediately knew she was a harlot. Everyone froze, wondering what her intention was, until they noticed a small bottle of perfume in her hand. She stood behind Jesus, not even daring to look Him in the face, and began to softly weep. Bending down, she opened the expensive perfume and poured it over His feet as her tears spilled over and ran down the Master's sun-bronzed, callused skin. Sobs wracked her body, for since she had heard Jesus speak to the crowds, she had been filled with shame and deep brokenness. *This Holy Man can help me. Perhaps He won't turn me away,* she pondered in silence, letting her actions speak the thoughts of her beating heart.

The Pharisee flinched, turning his head away from the sinful woman in disgust. *If this man were really a prophet,* he reasoned, *He would know who is touching Him. She is a sinner!*

Jesus broke the silence and spoke directly to the host. "Simon, I have something to say to you."

"Master, say on." The Pharisee gave a small bow of courtesy to disguise his inner contempt.

"There once was a certain banker who had two debtors," Jesus began in His storytelling fashion. "One owed him five hundred pieces of silver and the other fifty. When neither of them could pay the loan, he forgave them both. Which one do you think will love him more?"

"Why," Simon replied, "I suppose the one who was forgiven the most."

"You've rightly discerned this," Jesus responded, turning to the woman with utmost compassion. "Do you see this woman?" He asked, not taking His eyes from her. "Simon, when I entered your house, you gave me no water for my feet, but she has washed my feet with her tears. You did not anoint me with oil, but this woman poured her precious perfume on me." He gently took the woman's trembling face in His hands. "So I say to her that her sins, which are many, are forgiven."

A slight gasp echoed through the chamber. Who was this man to offer forgiveness of sins? Only God Himself could grant such a pardon! Jesus turned to those watching and declared with a slightly stronger tone, "She has loved much." Looking back to the woman, He smiled and said, "You are forgiven. Your faith has saved you."

Astonished, the woman could barely believe her heart had been heard. Jesus had not despised her or turned her away. Instead, He understood, honored her faith, answered her secret prayer. Lifting the woman to her feet, Jesus blessed her.

"Go in peace," He said and turned back to the meal. The shocked men around Him were silent as they pondered their own hearts. The fragrant perfume lingered in the air, reminding them all of the woman who had dared to bare her soul to the Master and had received the gift of grace.

True Beauty Tip

In the physical world, sometimes we mask our faces with beauty products in an effort to hide blemishes we would rather not own. What about "soul makeup"? Do we put on confident facades when our hearts are actually broken and empty inside? Sometimes such masks are necessary to bravely put our best foot forward and complete a task, but if a mask becomes a lifestyle—like a cosmetic we can't live without—then we need to check the health of our souls.

Even though we might feel vulnerable stripping off our masks, Jesus never despises our honesty. We never need fear beautiful vulnerability before the One who knows us deeply, inside and out. This means choosing to become healthy enough to live freely from the heart. We can run into the arms of our loving Father and trusted people who can help us get there.

Questions for Reflection

1. In what areas of your life do you feel vulnerable (perhaps your past, a "flaw" in your body, or a lack of performance in an area of your life)?
2. Do you think God thinks less of you because of these areas?
3. If you were to talk to Him about these areas, what would you say?
4. How do you think He would respond? Listen for Him to speak to your heart.

ten

Beautiful Dreams

Every great dream begins with a dreamer. Always remember, you have within you the strength, the patience, and the passion to reach for the stars to change the world.

Harriet Tubman

Sometimes beauty steps into our lives at unexpected moments, delightfully surprising us with an entrance we didn't see coming. One of these chance encounters took place in East Texas one evening as the suffocating humidity settled like a wet blanket on a small town. I was visiting my family in the area and volunteered to be keeper of the hot dog coupons at a community festival, so I threw on some denim overalls and helped corral floods of people toward an open barn. By the end of the day, clouds of billowing dust hung in the air from thousands of trampling feet, and I was looking forward to a hot shower. That's when I ran into Heidi, a friend from a church I attended when in town. Age twenty-five, with brunette curls piled up into a loose bun, she manned a double stroller while serenely watching her young boys romp in the festival remains. Heidi's ready smile and sweet disposition made our conversation easy. After a minute of small talk, her statement took me by surprise.

"You know, a couple years ago, Nathan and I were separated and I filed for divorce."

I had no idea—in fact, Nathan and Heidi looked like the perfect young couple. *Ah,* I thought curiously, *a beautiful tale is hiding here,* and I asked to hear more. So a few days later, we sat down after hours in an empty coffeehouse to film her story. In a soft voice, she shared the tender tale of a dream that had stretched faith and given her wings. Heidi's story reminds us that sometimes the dreams we long for the most come back around at the most unexpected times.

Heidi's Story

Raised in Ahuatlan, Mexico, as the daughter of missionaries, Heidi lived inside the church compound in a yellow school bus that had been converted into a mobile home. Childhood was simple, and her parents' church was a beautiful place where worship and the tangible presence of God grew like a sweet oasis in the Mexican desert. Heidi often saw God heal cancer and various sicknesses through her parents' ministry. Church was a solid community, the people were kind and wise, and the comforting presence of the Holy Spirit was always near.

However, persecution of the Christian faith was always a threat. On an average Sunday morning, women entered church with ugly bruises from their harsh husbands who opposed their church attendance, and drug cartels tried to hide in their congregation as cover for their trade. One day a man ran into church brandishing a gun, declaring that he was going to kill Heidi's father. Trembling with fear, Heidi raced to the car with her older brothers and hid under the seats, imagining the worst. Inside the church, her dad began to tell the gunman that God had a plan for his life and loved him. Eventually, the man crumpled at the altar, sobbing, "No one ever told me they loved me!" He ran outside and emptied his shots into the air. From her hideout in the car, Heidi heard the gunfire and thought, *Dad is dead! We're never going to see him again,* and fear quickly wedged itself into her innocent world.

In this simple yet dangerous world, Heidi's fair skin and blue eyes placed her under the threat of kidnapping, so she was constantly watched by her family and protected from possible predators.

A princess in a castle, guarded and isolated from the rest of the world, Heidi placed all her trust in the familiar faces around her. Enveloped in this protective bubble, she was never alone—yet always alone. Fear was normal . . . fear of being kidnapped and fear of being forever trapped in the smallness of her world. She dreamed about finding a Prince Charming and wondered whether anyone would ever ride into their small town to sweep her off her feet.

One man did, and he instantly changed her world with a tender crush. Nathan was a handsome, blond teenager with a dashing smile who melted Heidi's little heart at the age of nine. At a youth camp in the United States, her older brothers befriended this winsome stranger, not knowing that their little sister was curiously watching from a distance. Nathan had a passion for church, and even at the age of fourteen, he would spend his lunch break handing out tracts to students. Seeing Nathan's love for Christ made Heidi feel there might be another human being who could share the world she loved. Smitten, she secretly gathered her brothers' camp photos and cut out all the pictures of Nathan, hoping for the day they could meet. For the next eight years, Heidi prayed and even fasted for this young man as her puppy love grew.

"God, this is the man I want to marry. Save him for me and only me. Let him fall in love with me." In the whispered prayers of a child, God birthed a sweet, romantic dream in Heidi's heart.

Much to Heidi's excitement, Nathan came to visit her church as a guest speaker for her youth group when she was seventeen. He couldn't believe how she had grown up from that shy, freckle-faced little girl at youth camp, and soon he asked if she would be his girlfriend. Elated, Heidi believed all her prayers were coming true. After Nathan returned to the States, Heidi climbed atop the metal roof of her Mexican house every afternoon to get a phone signal to talk to her boyfriend. Six months later, he invited her to the US, where he proposed, and the happy couple got married.

A fairy tale unfolded as Prince Charming waltzed into the world of this Mexican missionary girl and swept her away. The white dress with billowing yards of satin, Heidi's long auburn curls gathered into a luxurious updo, Nathan looking as dashing as ever with his black tux and brilliant smile—it was a dream come true. It seemed heaven had responded to a little girl's prayers, and at age eighteen, Heidi walked down the aisle toward the man she loved.

Leaving the little Mexican mission, Heidi moved to the US with her husband to begin a new life. Suddenly, her head-on collision with culture shock began. The constant threat of violence was gone, but she didn't know how to handle life outside the bubble. With the fear of abduction still screaming in her ears, Heidi discovered that she couldn't even walk through a grocery store alone, and she didn't have a driver's license or know how to drive a car.

Nathan's a college graduate and is used to being with confident women, Heidi mused, wincing as she labored through her struggles. *He expects independence from me, but I don't even know how to buy groceries alone. I feel like such a horrible burden.*

Two babies in the first two years of marriage brought even more challenges to the young couple, and soon their marriage began to show signs of wear, cracking under pressures even Heidi couldn't see. She began to have nightmares that her husband was leading a double life, and the icy grip of fear began to reach its fingers around her heart. Not wanting anyone to think badly of Nathan, she told no one about her suspicions and silently waded through her life in a strange country with no one to confide in. Yet inside, she was pleading to be heard.

Her fears were finally confirmed when she learned that Nathan had fallen away from his faith and was deeply entrenched in a life of addiction. Heidi was crushed, and the hidden dam of emotional agony finally broke. No longer able to cope with the pain, she packed up her children, moved fourteen hours away to be with her family, and filed for divorce. The fairy tale dream had turned into an ugly nightmare, and she found herself wrestling with despair beyond anything she had ever experienced.

Heidi retreated to the comfort of her pain, and her grief became a personal companion. Her pain was her friend, a security— a place she could run to and hide. She stopped eating, completely wrapped in her grief and feeding the grief with her sadness. Her face soaked with tears, she wrestled with doubts, wondering why this was happening to her. Heidi cried out to God, recalling the prayers of the little girl in Mexico who had fallen in love with the smiling, blond boy.

"God, I prayed so hard for a relationship with Nathan, but now I wonder if I somehow made it happen on my own. Maybe this marriage wasn't from You after all. Maybe this was my dream and not Yours." One day she realized the knot of emotion in her chest was not making her the person she wanted to be. Nathan had been her hero, and she had expected him to be perfect and worshiped the ground he walked on. When he fell off the pedestal, she fell too, plummeting into despair. She realized this new companion called pain was leading her toward a slippery path of anger and bitterness, away from everything she knew that would bring truth and peace. Taking a deep breath, she turned to God and said, "Okay, it's just You and me, Jesus. You are my

Lover, my best Friend, my everything. I'm giving You my pain—I want You to carry it for me."

Heidi had always believed in God and had seen miracles as a little girl in church, but now she needed the tangible companionship of Jesus, and she realized the Friend who sticks closer than a brother was offering His hand to the trembling little girl who needed a caring touch. In her heart, Heidi turned slowly toward this offer of friendship and made the deliberate choice to turn away from her pain and toward Jesus. Her shattered dream was placed in the hands of the Dream Giver, and she clung to Him with stubborn hope that He would bring her through this trial.

As the slow awakening of her heart began, Heidi started feeling the quivering thrill of joy as Christ's love found a way into her life. Through a word from a friend, caring family members, and her own quiet times with God, the pain began to lift from her shoulders as her perspective changed. For the first time in her life, she was unafraid to be alone because she understood that God was with her. Instead of knowing *about* God, she began to *know* Him as a faithful friend and daily companion, and the bitterness of abandonment began to lift.

Several months into her journey, a strange thing happened: in His still, small voice, God began to speak to Heidi about giving Nathan a second chance. In her private wrestling match with God, she cried, "God, I don't think I can give Nathan a second chance. I'm afraid."

"That's right," the voice responded tenderly. "You can't love without Me. I know you can't love Nathan right now, but I want to love him. Let Me love him through you."

"Okay, Lord," Heidi said, closing her eyes and collecting every ounce of trust she had in her heart. "Because I love You, I'll do it."

Mustering all her bravery, she called Nathan and asked him out on a date. Little did she know that her husband had hit rock bottom and had cried out to God for help, abandoning his addiction and running to the counsel of his spiritual mentor. Broken and ready to make amends, Nathan drove fourteen hours to visit, and Heidi's hopes slowly began to rise. They both shed tears during that date, but this time the tears were over their parting at the end of the day, and neither wanted the weekend to end. After Nathan left, Heidi thoughtfully wondered if she could trust the dream that hesitantly fluttered like a phoenix underneath a pile of soot and ash. Could her dream actually live again?

With this question in her mind, one day Heidi read Isaiah 43:18–19:

> Do not remember the former things,
> Nor consider the things of old.
> Behold, I will do a new thing,
> Now it shall spring forth;
> Shall you not know it?
> I will even make a road in the wilderness
> And rivers in the desert.

"Heidi, will you allow Me to do a new thing with your relationship?" her Father whispered as the words jumped off the page and into her heart. Later that day, she discovered that she wasn't the only one God was talking to. Both her pastor's wife and her mother called and spoke of Isaiah 43:18–19. On the same day, her pastor called Nathan and shared the same verse! Heidi realized that God wanted to do a new thing—taking something completely broken and not just putting it back together like it was before but rather doing something completely new. The couple continued to receive counsel and slowly rebuilt their dream of life together.

When they renewed their vows a year after their separation, Heidi had a new confidence and a new shine to her eyes. This time she was living with eyes wide open, aware that Nathan was not a perfect person and neither was she, but they were both willing to help each other grow. She couldn't lean on others for emotional security: that was God's job. He was her ultimate Protector, Provider, and Lover of her soul. With full confidence in her heavenly Father, Heidi made her vows with this statement beating in her heart: some dreams need a second chance.

"I used to think that love fit snugly in a box with a nice little bow," she said with bold confidence shining in her clear, blue eyes, "but I learned that love can be messy. If you think about Christ dying on the cross: that was perfect love, and it was messy. I'm not expecting life to be perfect anymore because Nathan and I aren't perfect, but this time around we know each other's weaknesses and we're ready to help each other conquer them. Today I know who my battle buddy is, and I know we're fighting for the same thing."

Now the young couple runs a ministry that helps people whose marriages are in distress. I have sat at Heidi's house around a November campfire and held their three little boys, warmed by flames, and listened to Nathan's fiddle while the firelight danced in Heidi's eyes. They have learned that God's dreams are not always an easy road, but with prayer, patience, and willing hearts, He makes beautiful dreams come true.

But true beauty in a woman is reflected by her soul. It's the caring that she cares to give, the passion that she shows; and the beauty of a woman with passing years only grows.

—Audrey Hepburn

Photo Shoot

For Heidi's before photos, she penned the words ALONE, PAIN, and AFRAID. With piercing blue eyes and curly brown hair framing her face, she sat on wooden steps against crumbling brick walls and posed with her signs. The back alley smelled of garbage, and rotting leftovers were piled up against a chain-link fence—reminders

of ugly, unwanted things. I snapped photos of Heidi's porcelain face amid the debris, reminded of the broken roads nobody wants to walk. Then we walked out of that alley, leaving her signs in a trash heap.

For Heidi's after photos, she wore a white dress with layers of tulle, piles of petticoats, and a swaying hoop skirt. "Mommy, you look like a princess!" Heidi's little boys exclaimed with wonder as I styled her hair and makeup. I dressed Nathan in chain mail and a broad sword as a knight in shining armor. Then I took photos of the couple at a local rose garden, where stone arches entwined with roses made the perfect fairy-tale setting. The young husband and wife were a stunning picture of the Father's power to restore even the most broken of dreams in our lives.

My Story

Sometimes our dreams need a makeover. We think we know exactly what our dreams will look like, but when our hopes come crashing down, we feel as if God hasn't been faithful. This is a good time to step back and ask God to do a new thing.

One of my favorite hobbies is rummaging through thrift stores to find antique silver. Pitchers, teapots, candleholders, chargers—if I can find a vessel that looks like it fell out of a storybook, I am delighted. Many times the silver is tarnished and dull and sometimes nearly black from lack of care, but when I run it through a bath of tarnish remover, the surface is instantly transformed, and I have a fantastic treasure. Most people in our generation don't care for silver because it is heavy and requires too much care, but I love it. There is nothing like throwing a party and serving your friends off precious metal place settings that brilliantly gleam with a fresh, new shine.

Dreams are like silver. Sometimes they sit on a shelf and get tarnished. The beautiful thing is that what we call useless and burdensome, God calls treasure. He is so good at removing the tarnish and causing things to shine. New things are His specialty, and He loves resurrecting beautiful dreams.

God's Story (Gen. 37–45)

Joseph had dreams at the young age of seventeen—real dreams, the kind that paint pictures in your head while you sleep and are unforgettably wedged in your memory when you wake up. But his dreams were so fantastic that his brothers laughed hilariously at them.

"Here comes the dreamer!" they chanted. "Go back to bed, sleepyhead!"

The peculiar dreams continued, filling the teenager's thoughts with moving pictures by night and questions by day.

"In my dream," Joseph naively shared with his brothers, not realizing that they were looking for reasons to mock him, "the sun, moon, and eleven stars all bowed down to me."

"You've eaten sour milk!" his brothers laughed. "We're all older than you. Give us one good reason we'd ever bow down!"

His father, the patriarch Jacob, cocked an eyebrow and pursed his lips at the apparent meaning. "You're dreaming that your eleven brothers and even your parents will someday bow down to you? Son, you're thinking too much of yourself."

Joseph ducked his head in embarrassment at this rebuke from his father. Still, the dreams wouldn't leave his mind. He couldn't help wondering what they meant. *The sun, moon, and stars bowed to me. . . .* Some nights Joseph wrapped himself in the colorful robe his father had given him and stared at the starry heavens, daring to believe they would move for him.

Finally, his brothers had enough. They found Joseph alone and attacked him. Tearing off his beautiful coat, they bid him and his colorful dreams goodbye as a slave trader clapped irons on him and hauled him away to Egypt. The cries of the teenage boy did nothing to soften the angry hearts of his older brothers, and dusk set slowly over a broken family in the Canaanite hills.

Years passed, and Joseph became a man. Somehow his dreams never left—they just got bigger. He found he could also interpret others' dreams, and eventually this gift from God brought him to the palace of a disgruntled king whose nightmare wouldn't allow him to rest.

"I had a dream," said Pharaoh with a crease between his eyes and a sleepless slump in his shoulders. "They tell me you can interpret it."

Joseph stood with quiet confidence before the king. "I cannot do it," he confessed, a small smile creasing the corners of his mouth. "God will give Pharaoh an answer."

Joseph interpreted the dream with such accuracy that he both brought peace and received power. Pharaoh stood with his chin raised and scepter outstretched as he surveyed his court. "Can we find anyone else like this, in whom the Spirit of God rests?" Turning his gaze to Joseph, he said, "You shall be ruler over my household. Only my throne will be greater in power than you. I am making you an overseer of the entire land of Egypt."

During those days, Joseph forgot the dreams of his youth. The glitter and pomp of his new position along with the responsibility of caring for the nation removed any thoughts of his bitter past. Then one day famine swept all of Egypt and Canaan, and Joseph's brothers came to buy grain from Egypt. Bowing low in front of the keeper of the grain, the brothers had no idea that Joseph, their teenage castaway, was the man who was standing before them.

In a flash, Joseph remembered the old dream of his brothers prostrating themselves on the ground. Over thirty years had passed since his youthful dreams, and now they had sprung to life without any efforts of his own. Instead of running from his brothers or punishing them, Joseph decided on a series of tests that would reveal whether his brothers were sincere. Then slowly turning toward them with tears streaming down his face, he said, "Come near to me." As the frightened brothers gathered around this strange Egyptian, he said with a voice thick with emotion, "I am Joseph your brother, the one you sold into Egypt. Don't be upset or angry with yourselves that you sold me, for God sent me ahead of you to save your lives. Now I will take care of you during this famine."

So the dream came true, even though every impossible obstacle had been hurled at the dreamer. After each blow, a faithful God was working behind the scenes until finally the dreamer stood with wide eyes and a wondering heart as the dream came to pass.

True Beauty Tip

Daring to believe in our dreams is a beautiful thing. With faith and trust in God, even dreams we stopped hoping for can spring back to life. Maybe they will look different than we expected, but when God brings a dream to pass, it touches the world in a powerful way.

Questions for Reflection

1. What dreams have you seen fulfilled in your life?
2. Have you ever struggled with disappointment over a broken dream?
3. Do you tend to hold on to the pain, or do you trust that God is able to make something beautiful from it?
4. What are a few dreams you are still waiting to see God bring to pass?

eleven

Beautiful Creation

You weren't an accident. You weren't mass produced.
You aren't an assembly-line product. You were deliberately
planned, specifically gifted, and lovingly positioned on the
Earth by the Master Craftsman.

—Max Lucado

I bit my lip to keep from shouting with excitement as we drove around the Irish coast. As is the case with many other dreamers, Ireland had always been a bucket list destination for me, and the island was everything I'd hoped it would be. With the sea to our right and magnificent green hills on our left, my new friend Danielle shared romantic legends of mystics and poets as we coasted down the highway. A young Irish visionary, this creative powerhouse is the CEO of her own company, Manna Cards, which produces innovative greeting cards sold in over eighty shops in the United Kingdom, each with an original graphic.

175

After we pulled off the road into a small parking lot along the shoreline, I grabbed my camera gear, and we walked to a pier that stuck out like a finger into the ocean. In the background, a twelfth-century Norman castle stood proudly on the bank. Danielle brushed her auburn hair away from her face and confided in her Irish brogue, "This pier is one of my favorite places. I always feel at home when I'm near the sea."

That day all was quiet, but Danielle had witnessed firsthand the battles that had ravaged her country. As she honestly shared the difficulties within her national and personal history, I was intrigued to learn of the battles that had taken place on this iconic countryside. Ireland is full of mystics and warriors, and Danielle's story had both. Woven within the tale was a fascinating thread of God's creative design and His remarkable purpose for each of His children.

Danielle's Story

Ireland is a land divided between north and south, still dubbed "Protestant and Catholic," representing the loyalist and nationalist political groups. Danielle was born during a time called the Troubles, when Belfast, Northern Ireland, was barraged with guerrilla warfare and riots between the parties. Even though the forces labeled themselves Catholic and Protestant, there was really no link to spirituality within the parties. Yet by the time over thirty-five hundred people had been killed in the Troubles, the young generation on both sides was angry with religion. Danielle and others came to hate Christianity. *Why would I want anything to do with a religion that has torn my country apart?* she fumed.

Sometimes the violence hit close to home. One day Danielle's mom picked her up from school, and they were confronted by a mob of men in black ski masks blocking the road. Attacking the car in front of them, the terrorists pulled the driver from his seat and torched the car, setting it ablaze in the middle of the highway. Her mother immediately threw the car's gearshift into reverse and frantically backed the vehicle away from the madness. They escaped unharmed, but the close encounter terrified the young girl and reminded her of the terrible violence she associated with religion.

Coupled with her nation's instability was a growing difficulty at home: Danielle's father was ill with a rare disease called Wegener's Granulomatosis, which had been misdiagnosed by medical doctors. Father and daughter had always been close, fishing, playing

in the water, and enjoying the sea. When he suddenly passed away, the six-year-old child looked up to the stars and prayed, "Jesus, if You are real, please bring my daddy back." It seemed as though heaven was silent to her request, and she wondered, *If God is love, why did He take away my father?* No answer felt satisfying to her.

Chaos escalated during her teenage years when sharp-tongued family members accused her of being involved with drugs. Danielle tried to defend herself, but no one believed her. The worst blow came when they declared with pointed fingers, "Your father would be ashamed of you!"

Crushed, Danielle's young heart curled up, and she wanted to die. When they declared that she would never amount to anything, she started to believe them. In her grief, Danielle turned to the Irish Sea and found solace on the pier overlooking the vast waters. The setting reminded her of the sweet times she treasured with her father. Her dad loved the sea, and his goal was to become a marine biologist, so Danielle vowed to pick up that dream and fulfill it in his place. *The sea is my home,* she thought. *I feel close to my father here. I'll pursue his dream since he's not here to complete it.*

Determined to carry on his legacy, she finished high school and began a college degree in environmental science. She deliberately chose evolution classes in order to learn scientific facts and disprove Christianity, secretly hoping that science could erase the idea of God's existence. The theory of evolution seemed to justify her disappointments in life, and she mentally stored up facts to challenge Christians who dared to believe something she couldn't. If she couldn't receive God's comfort, she wanted to make sure no one else could either.

She landed a job after college as a conservationist on a tiny Greek island in the Mediterranean where a small group of conservationists lived in an olive grove. Every summer for five years, she lived in a tent, wore no shoes, and let the sun bake her light skin into a dark, bronzed tan. This was her getaway, far from the troubled nation of Ireland and the chaos of her family. The beauty was a healing balm as the scientists looked after sea turtles. Danielle and her group followed the massive turtles, tagged them, and kept their young hatchlings safe from uncaring humans. She taught the theory of evolution to tourists and even enjoyed having conversations with Christians to challenge their faith with scientific ideas. However, Danielle had no idea that the Creator she attempted to disprove was about to make Himself known.

Every September she left Greece and returned to face the harsh reality of life in Ireland. She had a boyfriend and good friends, but they couldn't cure the deep depression and anger that lurked just beneath the surface of her smile. One night she went to an illegal warehouse party in Belfast, drank a bottle of wine, and returned to her friend's house completely out of control. She smashed the mirrors and left such a terrible mess that her friend said, "Danielle, I don't know who you are anymore, but you really scare me."

Shame welled up inside Danielle; she had turned into the person she had been accused of being years ago, but she was terrified to admit it. Her mother drove her home and began to talk about God. Hung over and angry, Danielle raged, "Mom! How can you actually believe a scientifically disproven book written two thousand years ago? Be quiet!"

As they pulled into the driveway, a strange, unexplainable thought crossed Danielle's mind. It was in her thoughts yet as clear as any voice she had ever heard. Without explanation, a Higher Power invaded her space and simply said, "You need to break up with your boyfriend."

Strangely enough, she didn't question the thought; she just obeyed. She had been living with a boyfriend she truly loved and believed she would marry, but suddenly she knew she was supposed to call off their relationship. She walked into the house, made the difficult phone call, and broke up the relationship. Immediately, all her insecurities surfaced, and over the next three days, Danielle wrestled through intense panic attacks as she began to face her anxieties and survey her true self. Sleep eluded her, although she ached for rest and took many sleeping pills. This time science and medicine weren't able to soothe her fears or give her the inner strength she desperately needed.

Cigarette in hand, she stood by the back door, watching her mom hanging up the clothes to dry.

"You know, Danielle," her mom said with the fervor of an Irish warrior, "God has the power to break the strongholds of fear in your life. If you'll pray with me, He will take them away."

Anger welled up in Danielle, and something inside her snapped as she took two steps toward her mom as if to strike out in violence. She caught herself just in time, but the murderous rage in her actions stunned her. In a flash, she realized there was something uncontrollable inside her and she needed Someone bigger to help. She fell on her knees in the kitchen and screamed, "Mommy, I need Jesus! Help me, I need God!"

Her mom propelled her into the special prayer room in their house and led her in the sinner's prayer. Danielle didn't feel anything different in the moment, but she knew she had made a decision to follow Christ. Pulling out her phone, she texted all her friends with the message, "I am now a Christian, and I'm going to be living my life differently." All her contacts were secular evolutionists, so the news shocked them, and Danielle lost almost all her friends in one day. Her best friend called her, sobbing, and wondered what her decision would mean for their friendship, but at the end of the conversation, she confessed, "Danielle, you used to be the kind of girl who could walk into a room and light it up with your passion, and I don't see that fire in you anymore. If you think that Jesus is going to be the one to bring that light back, then I'm completely behind you."

Soberly, Danielle went to her room to think. Next to her bed was a pile of sleeping tablets. As she reached for the pills, the same clear heavenly voice stopped her. "You won't be needing those anymore."

Again, Danielle simply obeyed the voice for some strange reason. She slipped into bed, fell asleep as soon as her head touched the pillow, and slept for fifteen hours. When she woke, her heart was singing, and she realized something had inexplicably changed. She pulled up the first worship song she could find on the internet and began to surrender her life to the Lord Jesus, asking Him to completely take her heart and make it His. The Lover of her soul met her in a wild embrace, and soon Danielle was on her bedroom floor, pouring out her heart as she sensed the presence of God in a powerful way. She was suddenly aware that Jesus Christ was a real person, not just a fictional character like Santa Claus, and she had been made by the Creator: she was no random act of science. God had made her with a purpose in mind, and she couldn't wait to discover more about Him.

Danielle was baptized in the Irish Sea she loved so much and eagerly began to read the Scriptures. She realized that evolution was a theory, not a fact, and that God was her Creator and had made her as His special masterpiece. This revolutionized her thinking, and when she returned to the Greek island for her job, she began to lead people to Christ and baptize them in the

ocean. Unfortunately, this didn't go over well with her friends, and soon Danielle found herself alone.

Accepting the truth of God's existence was a major step, but stepping into her destiny took some time. Danielle realized that God was her Creator, but she had no idea He wanted to create beautiful things *with her*. This discovery began in the strangest of ways when her health began to deteriorate and she fought fibromyalgia and rheumatoid arthritis at the age of twenty-four. Pain plagued her body, so the doctor prescribed intense medications such as morphine and diazepam, and she took twenty-nine pain tablets daily to overcome the pain. Bound to a wheelchair, Danielle could only cry out to God. She lay on the family's prayer room floor, pleading, "Lord, please do something! My life has no purpose or meaning. I don't believe in my college degree anymore, because I want to give glory to You for creating life, not the theory of evolution. Besides that, I'm not well enough to work because I'm crippled. Still, I believe You made me for a purpose."

During her pain, the Scriptures became her treasure, and she started doodling pictures to go with the verses she was reading. Although she wasn't a great artist, she kept a little notebook in which to draw images when the inspiration hit. During her hours of worship in the prayer room, the sketches kept coming as the Creator God filled her heart with ideas.

One day Danielle went shopping for a greeting card to encourage a friend, but none of the selections appealed to her. Annoyed, she went into her prayer room and heard the still, small voice of her Savior speak: "I want you to start a greeting card company that will build the church with My Word, truth, and life."

"God, you've got the wrong person!" Danielle argued. "I don't know anything about graphic design, I have no money, and I'm not creative at all." Then she paused, wondering if this could possibly be God's will. "If this idea is from You, please send me a laptop so I can work on the designs," she added.

Shortly afterward, her mom rushed up to her, saying, "Danielle, a woman at church said that she received an unexpected inheritance and God told her to buy us a computer!"

Some of us have great runways already built for us. If you have one, take off. But if you don't have one, realize it is your responsibility to grab a shovel and build one for yourself and for those who will follow you.

—Amelia Earhart

183

Shocked and excited, Danielle received the laptop and began to experiment with card ideas, partnering her inspirational pictures with verses. It was laughable to watch the Creator she had denied for so long fill her with such wonderful artistic ability.

Creating graphics to go along with God's Word brought Danielle a sense of purpose even in her frail position in a wheelchair, but she was about to learn that the Creator had even bigger plans. While she was in the prayer room one day, a Scripture verse flashed through her mind, and she was reminded of Jesus's words to the woman who had been sick for eighteen years: "Woman, you are loosed from your infirmity" (Luke 13:12).

The words came alive as if they had been written just for her. She held the words in her heart, cradling them like a newborn child and believing that somehow God was going to get her out of the wheelchair. Willing to put feet to her faith, Danielle wheeled herself to the altar at every church service she attended and asked for prayer, but with no result. Sometimes the disappointment was almost unbearable, and she felt the sting of rejection each time it appeared her prayers had gone unanswered. Nevertheless, she tenaciously believed God would move and fulfill His promise.

About six months after her prayer room encounter, she went to a Christian conference and sat in her wheelchair while the band played. One of the worship leaders waltzed up to her with a spring in her step and said, "Hey, sweetie, can I pray for you?"

"Of course you can," Danielle promptly responded, and the young woman began to pray for healing. Danielle felt the familiar lump of disappointment choking her when nothing seemed to happen. "It's okay, God must be developing my character through suffering," she voiced out loud.

The worship leader responded, "Sweetie, God loves your character, but the Scripture passage you're thinking of is referring to

enduring persecution for your faith. God did not give you this disease," she affirmed. "You're believing a lie."

Danielle was shocked. Suddenly, she realized that the Creator had a plan, and He was not finished yet. Like the woman who touched the hem of Jesus's robe, she felt the love of God shoot through her body as the voice of her Father God said, "Woman, you are loosed from your disability. Run!"

Danielle leaped from her wheelchair and began to run around the tent where the meeting was being held, tearing off her metal support braces and holding them over her head as she ran for joy. Like the Pied Piper, the young woman was soon followed by a stampede of followers as half the audience began to run with her, praising God for the miracle in her body. Instantly, the pain was gone, and she has been completely well ever since that moment.

She went back to her rheumatologist and said, "I know this is going to sound crazy, but Jesus healed me."

Her doctor smiled sweetly, gave Danielle her business card, and told her to call if things changed. Danielle and her mom hung the card on the fridge, but they never used it because the young woman was completely whole.

Danielle returned to the pier that overlooked the Irish Sea. In the salty air and soft fog, she realized it was time to pursue the dream God had placed inside her: creating a greeting card company that would encourage others with His Word. She jumped into her greeting card business, using the graphics she had created while on the prayer room floor. The cards started gaining traction in the UK. Today they are sold in eighty-two shops, have been translated into other languages, and are sold in other countries. Now Danielle passionately shares her faith with infectious joy and causes everyone around her to rethink their own relationship with God. She recently shared, "It's not enough just to talk to God; you have to obey Him. Only then can you fully receive what He has made you to be."

Photo Shoot

I filmed Danielle's story on the pier that means so much to her, and then we drove up the Irish coast and stopped at beautiful locations to shoot her before photos. The words she chose to write on a small white notebook were BITTER, ANGRY, ALONE, and BROKEN.

Then we drove farther up the coast to a castle that inspired C. S. Lewis's depiction of Cair Paravel in the fantasy land of Narnia. Set on a small peninsula, the castle ruins were a delight to explore. I brought a red satin dress for Danielle, and she perched on a cliff with the Irish Sea at her back and held out her arms in joyful abandon. No longer trying to justify her existence or reason away her pain, she rejoiced that she was designed by the Creator of the universe and He had purposely made her to carry His love.

My Story

One of my favorite artistic mediums is clay, and I use my potter's wheel in front of an audience to teach how God shapes us into beautiful vessels. I love to transform a piece of clay with my hands and talk about the process our lives go through in the master Potter's hands. Sometimes I speak to a youth group, starting with a raw lump of clay that looks nothing like the finished product. Holding the ball of moist clay in front of the kids, I ask, "Do you think this piece of clay can become a beautiful vessel by itself?"

"No!" they respond with a shout and a laugh.

"What if I throw it on the ground a few times?" I offer, dropping the lump onto the cement floor. "Will that make something beautiful?"

"No, it will stay the same!" they chorus back.

"What if I left it alone for a million years, or maybe a billion? Would it become a beautiful vessel?" They laugh at the ridiculousness of the idea, and I respond, "You're right. The clay needs an artist." I place the clay on the wheel and spin it into motion. Then with intention and design, I press my fingers into the clay, and it begins to transform into a beautiful vessel. Within a few short minutes, a lovely pot has been created, and I ask the kids, "What about you? Your body, mind, and heart are incredibly complex. Do you think you just happened to be, or did your Creator God make you?"

I watch the mental lightbulbs go on as they realize that an artist was needed to purposely create the vessel on the wheel. How much more is a Creator needed to design the intricate shape of a human being! When we really think about it, the idea that we were somehow an accident or a product of chance and nature is simply ludicrous. Our value comes from the truth that God made us in His image and has a plan for our lives.

God's Story (Ps. 139:1–2, 6–8, 13–18, 23–24 TLB)

Under his breath, King David hummed a melody while unrolling the fresh parchment and dipping his reed in the inkwell to pen a new song. A wave of tender emotion caught him off guard as he pondered his past, remembering how God had called him as a teenager and preserved every step of his difficult journey. David's life had not been easy, nor safe. Yet today, addressing his new song to his chief musician, he wrote a personal prayer, which flowed from his pen.

> O Lord, you have examined my heart and know everything about me. You know when I sit or stand. When far away you know my every thought.

The king lifted his pen as memories flooded his thoughts. He recalled his days as an innocent harpist in the king's court and the spears that had nearly pinned him to the wall. Who could forget the battle against the massive giant? David sighed softly, as if breathing itself was an act of worship. The times he narrowly escaped death were too numerous to count, and the words of his new hymn spilled onto the page.

> This is too glorious, too wonderful to believe! I can never be lost to your Spirit! I can never get away from my God! If I go

up to heaven, you are there; if I go down to the place of the dead, you are there.

David recalled the difficult days of his youth, when his family sent him to pasture the sheep. Who could have guessed that God would call him to rule the nation? How could a God so large care for someone so overlooked, even by his own family? *God knew me far before I knew myself,* he reasoned. Even before his birth, the Creator had planned his life.

You made all the delicate, inner parts of my body and knit them together in my mother's womb. Thank you for making me so wonderfully complex! It is amazing to think about. Your workmanship is marvelous—and how well I know it. You were there while I was being formed in utter seclusion! You saw me before I was born and scheduled each day of my life before I began to breathe. Every day was recorded in your book!

How precious it is, Lord, to realize that you are thinking about me constantly! I can't even count how many times a day your thoughts turn toward me.

David's pen stopped once again, and his thoughts turned pensive. *What deep love the Creator God has for His creation,* he marveled. Determining that this great love should have a response, David pondered his own heart's deep cry. *Love like this,* he reasoned, *deserves the echoing tribute of my heart. I long to give back the love that has been given me.* Dipping his reed in the ink once more, David earnestly wrote the inner longing of each heart that has been truly touched by God's love.

Search me, O God, and know my heart; test my thoughts. Point out anything you find in me that makes you sad, and lead me along the path of everlasting life.

⁓

189

The same Creator who overwhelmed David with His love three thousand years ago is still deeply connected to His artistry today. Like a master craftsman in love with his work, God never stops caring about or being fascinated by His creation. He is constantly reaching out to fulfill the work He started when He wove us together in the womb, and He is so creative with each life that is surrendered to His plan. We are beautifully made and cared for—let's respond to His love by giving Him our lives.

True Beauty Tip

We are uniquely made by the God of the universe. We can embrace the fact that we are His beautiful works of art and that He is immensely proud of His creation.

Questions for Reflection

1. What does being God's creation mean to you?
2. Do you think the Creator loves His work, just like an artist loves a piece of art they are proud of?
3. You were created with a plan in mind. What are some ways you can pursue God's purpose in your life?

twelve

Beautiful Invitation

Your dignity can be mocked, abused, compromised, toyed with, lowered and even badmouthed, but it can never be taken from you. You have the power today to reset your boundaries, restore your image, start fresh with renewed values and rebuild what has happened to you in the past.

—*Shannon L. Alder*

"I wasn't broken because I was a stripper," Deanna declared with forthright honesty. "I was a stripper because I was broken."

A beautiful California blonde sat across from me, her long hair falling in soft curls around her face as she unwrapped the layers of her story. As we filmed in a mountaintop home that overlooked a panorama of desert hills, I asked her what led a promising young teenager who started college at the tender age of sixteen to invest her life in clubs as an exotic dancer. What brought her there, kept her there, and led her out?

191

There are no words to adequately capture our thoughtful conversation, and my best attempts feel like carrying fine wine in a paper cup. Her story takes us deep into the quest of every woman who craves love, beauty, and security for herself and her family. Deanna's story reminds us that God doesn't just want to change our lifestyle; He wants to invite us into a bigger love story than anything we could imagine.

Deanna's Story

The scene plays like a horror flick that should have been banned from all childhood eyes. Deanna was only three years old when her parents separated, and her first memory is of her father angrily leaping over the back fence to collect his belongings from their home. Through fearful eyes, she watched him attack the outdoor barbecue grill that was chained to the ground and try to drag it away while her mom shouted, "What are you doing? Get out of here!"

Grabbing her mother by the neck, he shoved her down the hall toward the bedroom and closed the door. Deanna and her older sister leaned against the wooden paneled door, listening to the violence on the other side.

"Go across the street and have the neighbors call the police!" her sister whispered frantically. Little Deanna ran as fast as her legs could take her, and soon officers appeared with a blaze of flashing lights to intervene in the domestic violence. She watched them take her father away, silently grieving as he disappeared from her life for the next few years. Slipping into the house, she found her mother alone, shaking with deep sobs brought on by the physical pain and humiliation of the episode. A piece of Deanna's innocence was stolen in that moment, and she started growing up a little too fast.

Several years later, her father remarried, and Deanna wrote him a letter while she was visiting him. "I really want some alone time with you," she penned, since life was busy and her girlish heart felt lonesome for her father. However, the invitation never reached him. Somehow her stepmother intercepted the letter and stormed down the stairs of their home. Instead of noticing a little girl who was desperate for her father's attention, she took the words as a personal rejection and screamed, "How could you want time with your father—without me?"

Shame welled up in Deanna. *How dare I want my father's undivided attention?* she thought, berating herself yet wishing for his company.

When Deanna was ten, her father was arrested and sent to prison, and Deanna ached to fill the vacant spot in her heart for a father's affection. Her mother worked nonstop to support the family, so Deanna was left to her own devices. She started having romantic relationships with boys at the age of thirteen and immediately became intimate with them. Self-respect for her body was pushed to the background, and she did whatever was necessary to feed her soul's craving for love, including experimenting with drugs. Between bullying at school and misunderstandings with teachers, she became a fighter—a girl who quickly jumped to her own defense if she felt misjudged by others.

After graduating from high school two years early, she entered college with the goal of becoming a physical therapist. One day at the age of eighteen, she went to pick up some drugs, and the seller's girlfriend walked through the door with a gym bag over her shoulder. She looked stunning, with perfectly styled

hair and amazing clothes, and Deanna couldn't suppress her curiosity.

"Did you just come from the gym?" she asked curiously.

"No, I just got off work," the young woman said, handing her boyfriend a large stack of money. "I'm a stripper."

Deanna was immediately intrigued. *Wow,* she thought. *This girl is so beautiful and hot. I want to be like her.* So Deanna started working as an exotic dancer, and at first the nights at the club were exciting. The atmosphere was electric, and she felt so beautiful in nine-inch stiletto heels. After each show, she was showered with compliments from men in the audience, and she thrived on the affirmation. *Finally,* she thought, *I'm gaining undivided attention from men.* Yet this euphoria wasn't enough to help her shrug off the unwanted emotions at the end of the day. She confided, "It's a vicious cycle—the women are after the money, and the men want to feel close to a woman. Even if the women are simply acting, it doesn't matter to the men: I fed off men's loneliness, and they fed off my brokenness. Nothing is free in the clubs—everything comes at a price. Even the job of dancing cost me dearly. I'm still suffering from back and neck pain from wearing tall heels and treating my body so poorly."

After coming home each day, the first thing she wanted to do was shower to wash off the lingering feeling of dirt. Money, passed through so many hands, felt filthy when she collected it. The compliments were shallow, and after the glitter and hype died down, she began to feel objectified as a woman. Still, the promise of affirmation and money had captured her attention, and she was determined to defend her lifestyle. After three weeks, she called her mom into the living room for a serious talk.

"Mom, I want to tell you what I've been doing. I know you won't like it, but I am not going to change my mind about this." Deanna squared her shoulders with an I-don't-care attitude and said, "I've been stripping at a club."

Her mother was outwardly reserved but realized her daughter was in crisis. She began to pray and continued to bombard heaven for the next five years as Deanna continued to work as a stripper. Those prayers would eventually penetrate the walls of a child still searching for her daddy, rescue her from her own damaged self-image, and introduce her to true love. But until then, the search for affirmation and personal security would only pull Deanna deeper into a career in which men tried to purchase her beauty instead of offering love without strings attached.

One day a TV show interviewed Deanna at a club, and the footage appeared on the evening news. Her aunt was horrified and emailed the entire family a link to the interview and the scoffing words, "Look at my niece. Shouldn't we be so proud?"

Deanna writhed with a sense of injustice. *You're trying to shame me and make me feel dirty and disgusting, but that's not the case!*

She kicked against the words that felt like condemning statements to her soul, and instead of compelling a change, the email made her pursue her job even harder. She married a man she met at the club and completely embraced the lifestyle of a dancer.

One day a group of women entered the club. Deanna thought they were lesbians, until word got around that the women were from a local church. They were kind and gracious, unlike any other Christians she had ever encountered, and offered her a gift. Deanna was mystified to discover lip gloss, earrings, and other cute items . . . until she saw a Bible in the package.

"We've got some Bible-thumpers tonight!" she warned the other dancers, rolling her eyes. When she got home, she shoved the cellophane-wrapped book into her closet.

Soon afterward, someone invited her to church for Easter, and since there were going to be fun activities after the service, she decided to attend with her mom, husband, and young stepson. During the service, Deanna listened to the pastor talk about the sacrifice of Christ. The suffering and deep love of Jesus touched her heart, and she began to weep uncontrollably. She had never experienced that level of love, and it stuck out like a beacon against the stormy gray life she had been living, but the response it demanded was too daunting to consider. She valued the money from her job, and walking away from it to follow Christ was too much to consider. *I've got this under control,* she thought. *God may be inviting me into His kingdom, but I'm saying no.* Facing her mom and husband, she declared, "I never want to come back here again!"

Still, she was curious enough to read books about Christianity. Sitting in the strip club, she read a story about a preacher who claimed to have experienced a terrifying encounter with hell. As she turned the final page, she slammed the book shut, shoved it across the table, and decided, *I'm just going to choose to disbelieve this whole religion thing, because if God exists, then hell exists, and I'm headed there. I'm not worthy to go knocking on heaven's door and ask for favors. I'll just forget the whole thing.*

Her life continued to get darker when a film producer came into the club and approached her about starring in a pornographic movie. Deanna was intrigued, but her husband was not.

"If you do that film, our marriage is over," he flatly stated.

"Well, then you can just leave," Deanna responded flippantly. "It's my choice, and I'm going to make it." She desperately wanted to be in control and to prove to the world that she could meet any challenge. She boasted the image of a woman who

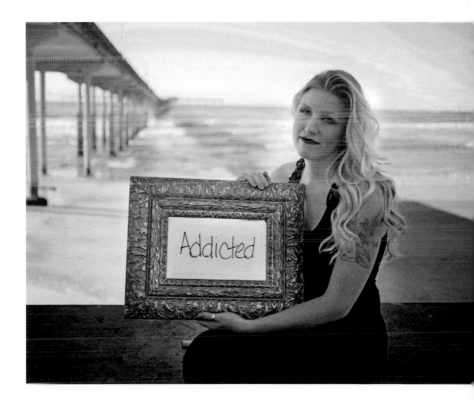

could handle life, made lots of money, and felt beautiful—all despite the little girl inside who desperately missed a father's care and affection. She lifted her chin and plunged back into life at the club, but before she could sign the film contract, a new chapter of her story began.

Despite her resolve, she found herself in church again, and this time the Savior's relentless love came rushing like a tidal wave to meet her. As she sat in the pew, the Father's voice began to speak to her heart. "Come to Me. Stop trying to run your life on your own. Just come to Me and let Me do this for you." Deanna started to cry as her Father in heaven extended a personal invitation: "I've got you, and I'll take care of you. I have so much more for you."

She walked to the front of the church and gave her life to Christ, tangibly feeling the Father's arms wrap around her. *My Father didn't bring me to church to tell me everything that's wrong with me*, she thought with awe as the tears ran down her face. *He's just glad that I'm here, and He wants me with Him.* Deanna felt a love bigger than anything she had ever imagined reach into her soul and heal the crack that had warped her self-worth for so many years. It was time for the fighter to become a little girl again, a daughter who didn't have to prove she was worthy of love but could come to the Father who already loved her. Her Father God always had time for her and would always provide for her needs. All He required was for her to accept His invitation and exchange His way for hers. As soon as she got home, she pulled the cellophane-wrapped Bible out of her closet. She held it to her

God's gifts put man's best dreams to shame.

—Elizabeth Barrett Browning

chest in awe, knowing it was a precious possession, and decided to choose God's way.

Quitting her job was risky, since many of the family's bills were paid with her income, but she decided to do it. She had never finished her degree in physical therapy, but she still loved the idea of helping people receive healing in their bodies. Miraculously, she was able to quickly complete the process of becoming a licensed massage therapist and found a job that paid the bills. Life took a different turn as she started putting Christ first and building everything else around Him.

One day a woman from church asked her to consider joining the group that visited strippers in clubs.

"I had a girl at the club sobbing in my arms last night, and I kept feeling you should have been there to speak into her life," the outreach leader shared. "Would you come with us and reach out to the girls?"

Deanna recoiled at the idea. The last thing she wanted to be was a pointed finger to the women in the club. Grimacing, she promised to pray about it, and when she sat down with her Bible, she kept feeling drawn to read the book of Jonah. Suddenly, it dawned on her that God was giving her, just like the Old Testament prophet, an opportunity to share His love in a place where doing so was difficult. *Jonah ran from God's call and ended up inside the belly of a fish!* she thought. *I won't run away like he did.* Excitement filled her thoughts as she realized that God had chosen her for this task. She remembered her slavery to money and how every compliment in the club had a handful of strings attached. What would it look like to walk back with an entirely different motive? This time she wouldn't be trying to gain her value or bolster her self-image; she would be carrying an invitation to her Father's love and giving it away for free.

One evening Deanna and several women from church went into a club and began to chat with the strippers. A strong sense of compassion welled up in Deanna as she saw the women in a completely different light. Before, the women had just been coworkers and sometimes even competitors who vied for attention and the chance to earn some cash. This time Deanna could see them through the eyes of her Father, and she began to see herself differently too. *These women are so deeply loved by Christ,* she thought. *I can feel His heart beating inside me. I must be so treasured by Him too!* Her entire view of herself began to shift as the Father's love became a mirror that reflected her true image back to her: she was chosen, wanted, and desperately loved by the God who promised to meet her needs. With a heart brimming with love, Deanna walked up to the women and said, "Hey, I just want you to know that the God of the universe, who created the heavens and earth, loves you with all His heart and wants a relationship with you. Nothing you could ever do will stop Him from pursuing you."

Receiving God's invitation of love had changed Deanna's entire world, and now she was extending that invitation to others too.

Photo Shoot

For her before photos, Deanna dressed in black leggings, a tank top, and her nine-inch stiletto heels. Posing on a cement wall by the California boardwalk, she held the words ADDICTED, DIRTY, BROKEN, and JUDGED written on a mirror.

For her after photos, I asked her to take the mirror to the ocean and let the water wash away all the darkly penned words from the surface. Wave upon wave scrubbed the glass until it shone

under the reflection of the setting sun. Then Deanna changed into a flowing white dress and wrote new words to describe the image she now saw in the mirror: REDEEMED and CLEANSED. Radiant with fresh hope, Deanna smiled, lighting up the beach as she reflected the Father's love.

My Story

To make the idea of God's invitation come to life, I decided to extend an invitation of my own. One day I invited several girls under the age of twelve to a tea party. The table was set with real china, flowers, and the most lovely place settings I could dream up. When the girls arrived, they excitedly chattered about the party, until I brought them to the table and said, "Welcome to tea! This beautiful party is for you. The only thing is you have to be dressed for the banquet."

A look of dismay swept over the girls as they looked at their everyday play clothes. "This is all we have!" they pleaded with obvious disappointment.

"You may not have brought party clothes," I responded with a small smile, "but I did. Come get dressed for the royal tea."

I opened my closets, and soon the girls were wearing frilly dresses and glittering costume jewelry as they paraded toward the table with chins held high, ready for the feast. After the merry sound of silver spoons clinking in china teacups died down, I shared with them the parable Jesus told about the wedding feast. All were invited to the king's wedding for his son, but people had to be dressed in wedding clothes in order to enjoy the feast. The king knew that not everyone would have royal garments, so according to the custom of the day, he provided robes at the door. If a person didn't receive his benevolence, they were ushered out of the feast.

"When you came today," I told the girls, "there was a place prepared for you, but you were not dressed for it, so I provided beautiful dresses for you to wear to enjoy the tea party. In the same way, God has so much planned for your life, but you have to choose His way and leave your 'old clothes' at the door. This is His invitation to all of us: 'Come to the party.'"

God's Story (Matt. 22:1–14)

The royal throne room buzzed with excitement as rows of servants assembled before the king, awaiting his word. For months, they had been preparing an extravagant wedding for the king's son, and now it was time to send out the invitations to the most lavish event in the kingdom. With a regal bow, a courier approached the king with pen in hand.

"Your majesty," he stated, "I am ready to take your dictation. Who do you wish to invite to the wedding?"

The king turned, and his eyes were both kind and wise as he met the courier's gaze. Considering the amount of time, labor, and investment that had gone into preparing for this celebration, the guests had to be chosen carefully and regarded worthy of such an honor.

"Invite the lords and rulers of the land," he declared. "My most trusted overseers will be invited to the wedding!"

Bowing, the servants left the throne room and immediately carried scrolls with the king's invitation to distant lands. Before long, they returned with dismay.

"Sire," the servants said with embarrassment. "The rulers refuse to come."

The king turned to face them with a look of disbelief. "What? They are my most trusted subjects. How could they refuse to attend the royal wedding?"

The silence was deafening, but the servants simply shrugged their shoulders.

"Go back to them again," the king said. "Perhaps there has been a mistake. Make it clear that they have been invited to the royal wedding. Everything is prepared. The dinner is ready, so come to the wedding feast!"

The servants bowed and left the palace, but some of them never returned. The evil landowners not only refused the invitation but also killed the king's messengers. The rest made excuses and went about their busy lives as if nothing had happened. Furiously, the king gathered his armies and avenged their lack of loyalty, ridding his kingdom of the insincere leaders. Then he called the servants and said with grief, "The feast is ready, but those who were bidden were not worthy. Now go and call the people off the streets so that my son's wedding will have guests."

As the servants left the court, one whispered to another, "Will the common people be able to find clothing suitable for the wedding? Surely they will not be able to afford such finery required for a feast like this!"

"Remember the custom of the land," replied the other servant. "If they have nothing suitable, we will be at the doors presenting them with fine robes from the king's own palace so they will be able to stand in his presence. Our king is both wise and kind—he will make sure everyone is able to enjoy the feast."

The day of the wedding arrived, and the entire kingdom was overjoyed. It was a royal party for everyone, and the guests were clothed in silk and velvet from the royal wardrobe. The king was happy that his lavish party was being enjoyed, and he stepped into the crowds to meet the guests. Out of the corner of his eye, he spotted a flash of gray. It looked out of place in this riot of royal color, so he moved closer to investigate. A man was sitting at the table clothed in a ragged suit that smelled like mothballs.

"Friend," the king said graciously, "how is it that you came here without a wedding garment?"

The man sputtered, but nothing came from his mouth. He had refused the royal robes at the door.

"Throw him out," declared the king. "I will only have people at my table who accept the honor of royal robes I offer them today. Many are called, but few choose to embrace the gift I give them."

Just like the wise king, God has invited us to His table, to something better than anything we could have come up with on our own, and He wants us to be part of it. Yet in order to receive what He offers, a makeover is required. He calls us royalty, so are we choosing to wear the garments of Christ's righteousness provided for us, or are we behaving like the man who tried to sneak into the feast without letting go of his old clothes? Are we embracing God's ways or clinging to our own?

Maybe the man with the old clothes thought he could figure everything out by himself. Perhaps he didn't want to bother the king or was trying to save the royal budget from an added expense, but the king took his refusal as a personal offense. In the same way, we have the option to try to figure life out on our own or to embrace what the King of Kings says: "You are beautiful, and you've been chosen with a high calling to do great things in My kingdom. You are fearfully and wonderfully made, and no matter what difficulties come your way, I am able to forgive and give you a brand-new start. Come to My table, and take off the old rags of your way of doing things. Accept My invitation and join the feast."

True Beauty Tip

When we accept the invitation of Christ, we become part of something far bigger than ourselves. Not only does He remove our sin and mistakes, but we are also empowered with strength to achieve things we could never accomplish on our own. Accepting the invitation to become His daughter is a beautiful thing.

1. Have you accepted Christ's invitation to the wedding feast?
2. Are there any ways you are trying to hold on to an old identity like the old clothes of the man at the wedding feast?
3. In what areas do you need to surrender to Christ and ask for His perspective?

Conclusion

*Though we travel the world over to find the beautiful, we must
carry it with us or we find it not.*

—*Ralph Waldo Emerson*

Discovering true beauty is a lifelong quest, and there are always
more adventures that bring fresh insight to ponder. While writing
this book, I found myself thrust into two very different situations
that reminded me that discovering beauty is not an end in itself;
it is the beginning of a brand new chapter.

Recently, I traveled through Ireland and Scotland to release a
docudrama I had created about the spiritual history of the Celtic
nations. It was a whirlwind: I stayed in castles and damp stone
mansions in the Highlands and islands while showing the film
to churches and groups. Every day of that monthlong trip was
packed with mountains to climb, ferry trips to remote islands, and
winding roads that gave way to spectacular views. While driving
over two thousand miles with my team, we often stopped the van
on a whim to explore some hidden glen or incredible vista, and

We do not want merely to see beauty. . . . We want something else which can hardly be put into words—to be united with the beauty we see, to pass into it, to receive it into ourselves, to bathe in it, to become part of it.

—C. S. Lewis

I practically lived with my camera in hand. At the end of thirty days, I was exhausted but exhilarated.

Just before leaving the UK, I received a message that my father was being rushed to the emergency room after taking a bad fall at his home in Texas. My heart dropped to my toes. Frantically, I rallied family members, and we made arrangements for his care after I made international calls and talked with his doctors. After his health stabilized, my family assured me that there was no need to rush back. So a few days later, I caught my flight from Dublin, traveled twenty hours back to California, and dragged my jet-lagged body to Texas the following morning.

It was surreal—trading the wild Irish Sea for a hospital room with stale air, bland food, and fluorescent lights—yet there was no place I would rather have been than at the bedside of my father. There was nothing stimulating about the environment, and the only photos were selfies with my father, whose pale face blended in with the bleached sheets, but at that moment, love was the most beautiful thing in the world. For me, that quiet room was the most compelling place in the universe, not because of what it brought me but because of what I could bring to it. In caring for my dad and simply being there, I brought a unique stability and comfort simply because I was my father's daughter and I had chosen to be present when he needed me. The experience was tiring, often boring, emotionally draining . . . and beautiful.

These two experiences reminded me that true beauty is twofold. First, we discover it for ourselves, and second, we give it to others. As we discover the depth of our identity in Christ, we grow in confidence and can give to others in a powerful way. Our Father in heaven aligns our lives with those of others so we can pour hope and life into them, just as I did in the hospital room with my dad. This doesn't undermine our identity; rather, it is an opportunity to share what we have in a unique way.

Jesus gave us the perfect example when He washed the disciples' feet. Completely secure in His identity, He was fully free to love others even on the night He was betrayed. Knowing the Father's love enabled Him to give it in a beautiful way. I love how the New Living Translation conveys this story:

> Jesus knew that the Father had given him authority over everything and that he had come from God and would return to God. So he got up from the table, took off his robe, wrapped a towel around his waist, and poured water into a basin. Then he began to wash the disciples' feet, drying them with the towel he had around him. . . .
>
> After washing their feet, he put on his robe again and sat down and asked, "Do you understand what I was doing? You call me 'Teacher' and 'Lord,' and you are right, because that's what I am. And since I, your Lord and Teacher, have washed your feet, you ought to wash each other's feet. I have given you an example to follow. Do as I have done to you. (John 13:3–5, 12–15 NLT)

Jesus modeled what it looks like to be a whole, confident person who chooses to love. The passage above begins by reminding us that Jesus knew what the Father had given Him and that He had planned a future for Him. He knew where He came from and where He was going, and nothing could dissuade Him from this knowledge. Such a strong confidence had permeated His soul that He bent down to serve others without the least bit of insecurity. As water splashed over the men's dusty feet, the Savior brought a refreshing touch to their callused skin, and He encouraged them to offer this service to others.

This passage also reveals that even though Jesus knew He would be misunderstood and crucified in just a few short hours, He didn't use His last night with His disciples to defend Himself or to convince them of His authority. Instead, His inner security came from a place no one could violate or steal away: His relationship with the Father. So instead of trying to impress His followers or make Himself feel good, He washed their feet. Humility was easy for Jesus because He was firm in His identity and could freely give Himself to others.

This powerful story reminds us of an important truth: beauty is not just for ourselves—we are called to give it away. Just like Christ, we also can become secure in the Father's love and freely give it to those around us. So let's look back at the previous chapters to see how we can apply the truths we have learned to serve others. Beauty is for us to discover and for others to find as we give it away.

Beautiful Security. As you grow in security as a woman who is deeply loved by our Father, in what ways can you create a secure place for others? Maybe you can help a child feel safe when they feel threatened by the emotional pressures of their peers, or perhaps you can take a meal to a family in crisis to bring stability during a season of turmoil. How can you create security for those around you?

Beautiful Daughter. Whether you are married or single, there are so many "daughters" in our world who need to be reminded that their true Father deeply loves them and desires a relationship with them. Is there someone you can send a note of encouragement to? Perhaps a young woman in your life needs a friend or a listening ear. Let's take a moment of our busy lives to reach out and remind someone that she is a beautiful daughter of the King.

Beautiful Adventure. What adventure can you create to help other women connect with true beauty? Maybe you can create a special lunch for your daughter and her friends, and after everyone has eaten, you can share your personal testimony of how you discovered Christ's love. (Keep it short and concise, and you will keep their attention, but be willing to answer any questions.) In my backyard, I have a table and chairs set up in the orchard where I host "Jesus parties." I spread a feast for friends and then pray for everyone afterward. The guests often share heartfelt prayer requests in this beautiful setting, and we enjoy the fun of eating outdoors too.

Beautiful Already. Celebrate someone else's uniqueness. Give a little gift to a friend simply because you saw something in a shop window that was perfect for them. Write a note of encouragement listing three things you appreciate about them and mention that you have been praying for them. Give an extra hug to remind them why you love them. Find someone who could especially benefit from such an act: a woman in a nursing home, a teenager from a broken family, or a pastor's wife who is constantly giving to others. Remind them how beautiful they already are—just by being themselves.

Beautiful Worth. One of the ways we can release value to others is by choosing our words wisely when we speak about other women. Our culture offers plenty of opportunities to compare, criticize, and envy, and it is easy to allow our conversations to devalue the women around us. Ask God to give you eyes to see others the way He does, and ask yourself, "Am I speaking about women based on their value in Christ, or do my words tear others down?" Ask the Father to show you how to value others with your tongue and reflect how He sees them.

Beautiful Trust. In a culture in which social media offers us thousands of followers, you would think that deep friendships would come easily. However, close relationships in our culture are often illusive because of this missing ingredient: trust. We have an incredible opportunity to offer trustworthy relationships that are grounded in God's love. So ask yourself, "Am I a trustworthy person? Do I break confidence on personal matters, hold grudges, or take people in my life for granted? Am I cultivating the art of listening to others, offering love with no strings attached, and giving from the heart?" Ask the Father to show you how you can be a person others can confide in.

Beautiful Exchange. Christ exchanges His hope for our despair, beauty for ashes, and comfort for mourning. As His children, we carry His voice of love to the world. Ask the Father how you can help someone exchange their pain for His peace. Perhaps you can write a note with a Scripture passage that speaks to their situation, buy them coffee and listen to their heart, or simply give them a hug and let them know you are praying. Christ's voice of hope can come through you.

Beautiful Warrior. There are so many ways we can go into battle for others. One of my favorite weapons is prayer. Nothing is as terrifying to the enemy of our souls as when we hit our knees and begin to intercede for our families, friends, and nation. Developing a life of prayer is a powerful way you can fight for those around you.

Beautiful Vulnerability. One of the keys to releasing beauty is being real with our own difficulties. When we allow people to see our shortcomings and let them know we are working at following Christ more closely, we immediately create an opportunity for conversation about matters of the heart. Allowing people to see our true lives—struggles and all—actually makes people take us seriously because they can relate to us more. Are there any relationships or ministries in which God can use the honest story of your journey to encourage others?

Beautiful Dreams. We all have dreams, so how can you encourage someone to dream big and explore their potential? If you are athletic, maybe you can run a 5K with someone who has never run one before or become a gym partner to help a friend achieve their fitness goals. Perhaps you can support a young adult who is planning a mission trip and invest financially to help them with their travel needs. Maybe you can create a vision board with your family using magazine clippings that represent what you would love to see happen in the next five years and then pray and work with each other to accomplish the goals. Dare to help others' dreams come true.

Beautiful Creation. Art is a powerful way to communicate beauty. Not only is it relaxing for you, but it can also be a great way to bless someone else. If you like to draw, create a picture and give it to someone with the words "This made me think of you because

_____." Write a poem or paint your own greeting cards. Even snapping a photo of a beautiful sunset and sending it to a friend with an inspirational message can be encouraging. Use your creativity to encourage others.

Beautiful Invitation. This is the best way we give beauty: by extending the invitation of Christ's love to others. After we join the family of God, we get to tell others how amazing it is to follow Christ. Each of us should be ready to share our own story; talk of Christ's power to save people from death, lies, and hopelessness; and offer His promises of hope and healing to those who accept the invitation.

My prayer is that this book encourages you to run after Christ's love with abandon. Know your identity and enjoy the life God offers you, and then become a carrier of that beauty for others. The more we embrace the beauty Christ gives us, the more we can become a conduit that true beauty flows through to impact the world we live in today. May you not only find beautiful but also let it overflow to others as you share it with a world that longs for authentic beauty. God bless you, my sisters, as our beautiful journey continues.

Acknowledgments

Thanks to Lucie, Brittny, Lauren, Karla, Kat, Amy, Lizbeth, Oriel, Charla, Heidi, Danielle, and Deanna for boldly sharing their journeys with the world. Your courage is inspiring.

Special thanks to Ruth, my literary agent, for long talks to brainstorm and refine the vision of this book. These pages exist only because you believed in our stories.

I am ever grateful to Rebekah Guzman and the team at Baker Publishing Group for working with me to share the message of true beauty with the world. Let's do this!

A storyteller and adventurer, **Rebecca Friedlander** uses the creative arts, film, and pottery to inspire and equip audiences with truths from God's Word. She has been in full-time ministry for fifteen years, ministering both locally and internationally. Her production *Radical Makeovers* is a TV series about beauty, featuring makeovers and testimonies of thirty women from around the world who have overcome image-related issues. The show inspired this book. Rebecca lives in San Diego, California. Connect with her at RebeccaFriedlander.com.

Learn more about Rebecca's art, storytelling, and adventures at
RebeccaFriedlander.com

❦

Subscribe to her weekly devotional, read her blog, and much more!

 RebeccaFriedlanderProductions

RebeccaFriedlander

RebeccaFriedlanderProductions

REBECCA FRIEDLANDER

GET INVOLVED WITH REBECCA'S WORK!

To learn more about *Radical Makeovers* and other TV shows, visit
RebeccaFriedlander.com/RadicalMakeovers.html

To purchase fine art prints or CDs, visit
RebeccaFriedlander.com/Store.html

To learn more about booking Rebecca
for Potter & Clay or Worship Leading, visit
RebeccaFriedlander.com/Booking--Contact.html

LIKE THIS
BOOK?
Consider sharing
it with others!

- Share or mention the book on your social media platforms. Use the hashtag **#FindingBeautiful**.

- Write a book review on your blog or on a retailer site.

- Pick up a copy for friends, family, or anyone who you think would enjoy and be challenged by its message.

- Share this message on Facebook: "**I loved #FindingBeautiful by @RebeccaFriedlanderProductions // @ReadBakerBooks**"

- Share this message on Instagram: "**I loved #FindingBeautiful by @RebeccaFriedlander // @ReadBakerBooks**"

- Recommend this book for your church, workplace, book club, or class.

- Follow Baker Books on social media and tell us what you like.

 Facebook.com/ReadBakerBooks

 @ReadBakerBooks